Diagonal (or On-Point) Set

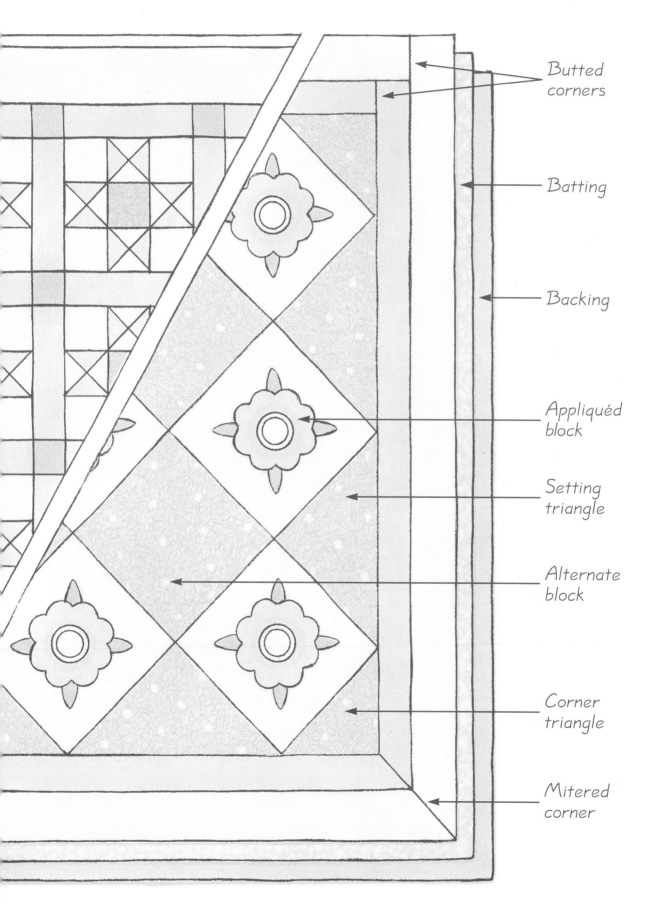

Butted corners

Batting

Backing

Appliquéd block

Setting triangle

Alternate block

Corner triangle

Mitered corner

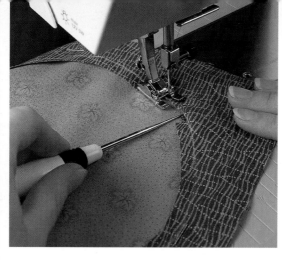

Rodale's Successful
Quilting Library®

Innovative Piecing

Sarah Sacks Dunn
Editor

RODALE

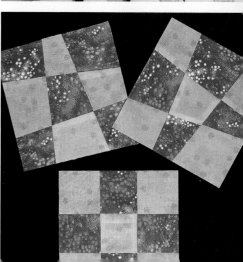

RODALE

WE INSPIRE AND ENABLE PEOPLE TO IMPROVE
THEIR LIVES AND THE WORLD AROUND THEM

The writers and editors who compiled this book have tried to make all of the contents as accurate and as correct as possible. Illustrations, photographs, and text have all been carefully checked and cross-checked. However, due to the variability of personal skill, tools, materials, and so on, neither the writers nor Rodale Inc. assumes any responsibility for any injuries suffered or for damages or other losses incurred that result from the material presented herein. All instructions should be carefully studied and clearly understood before beginning any project.

Printed in the United States of America on acid-free ∞ , recycled ♻ paper

We're always happy to hear from you.

For questions or comments concerning the editorial content of this book, please write to:

Rodale Inc.
Book Readers' Service
33 East Minor Street
Emmaus, PA 18098

Look for other Rodale books wherever books are sold. Or call us at (800) 848-4735.

For more information about Rodale and the books and magazines we publish, visit our World Wide Web site at:
www.rodale.com

Book Producer: Eleanor Levie,
    Craft Services, LLC
Art Director: Lisa J. F. Palmer
Editor: Sarah Sacks Dunn
Writers and Samplemakers:
    Sonya Lee Barrington, Karen Combs,
    Judith Doenias, Karen Eckmeier, John Flynn,
    Barbara Olson, Jackie Robinson,
    Elizabeth Rosenberg, Linda Dease Smith,
    Karen Costello Soltys, Carol Taylor,
    Elsie Vredenburg, Virginia A. Walton,
    Darra Duffy Williamson, and
    Cheryl Wittmayer
Photographer: John P. Hamel
Illustrator: Mario Ferro
Copy Editor: Erana Bumbardatore
Indexer: Nan N. Badgett
Hand Model: Melanie Sheridan

Rodale Inc.
Editorial Manager, Rodale's Successful
    Quilting Library: Ellen Pahl
Studio Manager: Leslie M. Keefe
Manufacturing Manager: Mark Krahforst
Manufacturing Coordinator: Patrick T. Smith
Series Designer: Sue Gettlin

On the cover: Detail, Skewed Hearts, by
    Elizabeth Rosenberg
On these pages: Attic Treasure, by Ellen Graf
On the Contents pages: Crescendo, by
    Karen Eckmeier

**Library of Congress
Cataloging-in-Publication Data**

Innovative piecing / Sarah Sacks Dunn, editor.
    p.   cm. — (Rodale's successful
    quilting library)
    Includes index.
    ISBN 1–57954–330–8 (hardcover)
    1. Patchwork. 2. Quilting. I. Dunn,
    Sarah S. II. Series.
    TT835.I56   2000
    746.46—dc21   00–044568

Distributed in the book trade
by St. Martin's Press

2 4 6 8 10 9 7 5 3 1 hardcover

Contents

Introduction 6

20 Top Tips
for Creativity 8

Simply Sizing Things Up . . .10

Strip Sets: About Face 14

Adventurous Settings 20

Off-Kilter
but On-Target 26

From Rectangles to Stars . . .34

A New Look
from Attic Windows 38

Show-Stopping
Pieced Appliqué 44

Easy Pieced Landscapes 50

Take a Picture,
Make a Quilt 56

Deep Space
Checkerboards 62

Throw Tradition a Curve . . .68

A Quick Route
to Drunkard's Path 72

Strip Piecing
Random Curves 78

Topstitched Curves 84

A Feathered Sun
to Let You Shine 92

Triumphant Arches 96

Outstanding
Prairie Points 102

Dimensional Patchwork . . .108

Tessellations:
Just Ducky! 114

Innovative Piecing
Glossary 120

Acknowledgments 123

About the Writers 124

Resources 126

Index 127

Introduction

I know what you're thinking. You're wondering if this is some "innovative" way to prewash fabric, right? Well, before I address that, let's talk about what makes something innovative. This book is about innovative piecing, which means that we looked far and wide for quilters who gave a new twist to an old technique and who march to a different drummer when quilting.

A Four Patch certainly isn't anything new; it's one of the oldest, most traditional patterns around. However, combining three different sizes of Four Patch blocks creates excitement, secondary patterns, and the illusion that your quilt is more complex than it really is. And simply folding fabrics into triangles can create kites, flowers, and stars, à la Jackie Robinson. These techniques, and at least a dozen others in this book, all have one thing in common. The quilters who perfected them thought outside the box, pushed the envelope, and then, when they found something they liked, tried approaching it from yet another direction.

Sometimes innovation strikes when we least expect it. A good example is Carol Taylor's quilt on page 14. She had a quilt top she'd sewn but didn't like, so she thought, "What the heck?" When she sliced it into strips and put it back together, she created a hot new design, appropriately titled "Wildfire."

If you're looking for a new angle on tradition, just peek at Karen Combs's angled Attic Windows design on page 38, or Barbara Olson's receding checkerboard on page 62. Or, try redrafting traditional blocks so they slant, sway, and skew their way right into a wonderful quilt that practically designs itself (see page 26).

Do you love the work of artist M. C. Escher? Design and then piece your own tessellating (interlocking) designs, courtesy of Judy Doenias. Her creation, at right and on page 114, is just ducky!

And curves...do we have curves! Modify the humble triangle square as Virginia Walton does, and suddenly you've got grace, movement, flair—with only a little more effort than the original block involved. (Check out page 68.) Sonya Lee Barrington shows how to cut and sew smooth, gently curving seams. Karen Eckmeier topstitches her curves, bringing a touch of appliqué into play; she also shares her technique for sewing arches, steep curves that still lie flat. And if you've always wanted to make a Drunkard's Path quilt but were intimidated by all those tight curves, Karen Soltys shares a technique borrowed from appliqué, to make units four at a time!

Have a stack of favorite fabrics you want to use without cutting them into tiny pieces? Arrange large pieces in an interesting, asymmetrical but balanced composition with a log cabin or jigsaw puzzle set. (See page 20.)

All this brings me back to the question at the beginning of this introduction: What *am* I doing in a tub full of fabric? I'm

seeking inspiration, of course! I play many roles in my life, among them editor, mother, wife, friend, volunteer, mentor, and quilter. This leaves me precious little time to be creative. The few moments I have all to myself are often when I am in the bathtub; that's when I imagine all the fun, exciting, new quilts I could start next. And sometimes, immersing myself in fabric (figuratively, of course) and removing myself from the real world helps me come up with a brand-new technique of my own. Try it!

Happy innovating!

Sarah Sacks Dunn

Sarah Sacks Dunn
Editor

20 Top Tips for *Creativity*

1 The first rule for creative thinking and designing is: Ignore the rules! Draft a block or a quilt top, but then design outside the lines and think outside the box (or triangle, or rectangle). Innovative ideas often emerge when you think about something old in a new and different way.

2 Your inner child has the freshest and most creative ideas—let that child out! If you don't have children to play or design with, borrow a friend's children or grandchildren. Provide plenty of colored pencils and graph paper. See what kind of blocks or quilts each of you come up with using the gridded paper.

3 Play with colored paper. Cut geometric shapes from various colored papers and use a glue stick to glue them to graph paper. Use this as the basis for a quilt design.

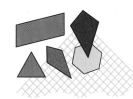

4 If you're stuck in a creative rut, take a hike! Step out of your sewing room and into the great outdoors. Inspiration comes most easily when you're relaxed and renewed, and Mother Nature is the greatest relaxer of all.

5 Look to nature for inspiration. Examine the veins on a leaf, the long shadow cast by a willow tree in the late afternoon, a spider's web, and even stones along a river's edge. Open yourself up to possible new patchwork designs that exist there. Watch for new color combinations, and seek out colors that you wouldn't have thought about using in a quilt.

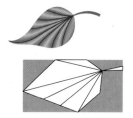

6 Create an "Inspiration Book" that contains images that appeal to you. Include magazine clippings, favorite quilt designs, colorful postcards, and works of art. Jot down notes on each page about what makes each image you've chosen appeal to you.

7 Keep a small sketchbook with you at all times to record your daily discoveries. Fill it with drawings and doodles, making an effort to add a new one every day. Include middle-of-the-night thoughts and inspirations, as well as the random ideas that pop into your head outside of your sewing room. Flip through your sketchbook for ideas and inspiration as you're designing your next quilt.

8 Take a class. Go to a quilt show. Even if you've been quilting for several years, you never know what new techniques or design inspiration you may uncover. Try to learn just one new thing that you can apply to a future project, and the class or show will have been worthwhile.

9 Experiment in your sewing room. Set aside some time just to play, using all those fabrics that you'd never put into a quilt. Combine colors you normally wouldn't, or piece a block or pattern you've been hesitant to try. You might discover a new way to do an old technique—now that's innovation!

10 For your next project, brainstorm, either by yourself or with friends (they

don't have to be quilters, just people who will toss lots of ideas on the table). Start with a chosen color palette, block, or special fabric. Have a "no criticism" rule, so each idea gets considered. Then, go back and sort out the best ideas to take to the design level.

11 Puzzle it out. If there's something you really want to do, try to figure out ways to make it work for you. Consider foundation piecing, making templates, or even appliqué to get the pieced look you're after. A problem-solving approach is often a great way to come up with new ways of doing things.

12 Put a spin on a traditional square block by redrawing it as a rectangle, circle, or diamond. Draw it with curved lines instead of straight; combine two or more patches into a larger piece.

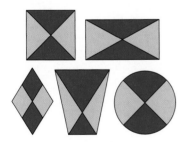

13 Acquaint yourself more with colors and how to use them. Choose a color, then search out photos and advertisements that feature that color. Make a collage or booklet, and note all the different values, tints, and tones of just that one color. Study how designers use your chosen color, and what other colors they use with it.

14 Keep your eyes open to inspiration from the masters. Look at art books and visit galleries and museums to see the work of famous artists. Go to an art school and observe the works of budding artists as they develop their own styles. Simplify your favorite painting for a patchwork version.

15 Wander through fabric shops, home decorating stores, and paint stores. Collect fabric swatches, paint chips, and wallpaper samples to combine and recombine in endless variations for innovative color schemes, patterns, and quilting designs.

16 Observe the manmade environment around you: the architecture of homes and buildings, roof lines, windows, fences, and furniture, right on down to the patterns of tile and parquet floors. Search for design inspiration everywhere, and visualize a patchwork version of these shapes. Keep your mind open to the limitless possibilities for design.

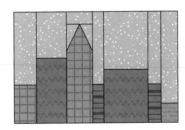

17 Listen to your favorite music as you design. As an alternative, listen to music you don't usually choose. Hold on to the feeling you get while listening, and translate that into a design or use it to choose colors. Just be sure to turn it up loudly enough so that you can hear it over the eventual humming of your sewing machine!

18 Let the fabrics speak. Collect a group of your favorite fabrics, and arrange and rearrange them into different compositions. Cut patches or shapes from them, and play with different combinations of shapes, colors, and forms.

19 Look to the past for inspiration. Study antique quilts, in which necessity was often the mother of invention. Make it necessary to invent or make do by giving yourself rules to work within, such as using a limited amount of fabric, choosing only from the fabrics in your scrap bin, or confining yourself to certain colors.

20 Blend unrelated concepts into the same quilt. Use fabrics that don't "go" together, or blocks of different sizes, shapes, or themes. The unexpected element in a quilt can be very interesting; it makes people stop and take a second look. Just make sure you include "resting places" for the eye.

Simply
Sizing Things Up

Many quiltmakers love recreating the tried-and-true patchwork blocks of our foremothers—with beautiful results. You don't have to abandon that tradition in order to be innovative. Play around with blocks of different sizes, substituting patchwork blocks for plain squares, or adding complexity by echoing one block inside another. Just a little spin on tradition can make a world of difference in your next quilt.

Getting Ready

Have your fabrics washed, pressed, and ready to cut and sew. Before you take that first slice into your fabric, take some time to play around with some ideas on graph paper. If you have the appropriate computer software, you can do your quilt designing on screen, enlarging or reducing designs with ease. Create blocks on paper or on the computer, and see what happens when you divide squares into pieced units. You'll be making the blocks look more intricate, but they'll remain just as easy to piece. Start with the ideas presented in the steps below, and then branch out; set the blocks in different ways, and check out the different looks and secondary patterns that result. Use a sized-down version of a block for sashing or a border corner unit, or sew blocks into strips for a pieced border that beautifully echoes your repeat block. Also consider making a huge, sized-up version of a featured block from your quilt to use as your backing!

Sizing Up a Four-Patch

Start with one of the most basic patchwork blocks. **A Four Patch block is made of four same-size squares in a two-by-two formation.** You can make the squares any size you want; just be sure to add ½ inch (for seam allowances) to your finished size. For instance, if you want each finished patch to be 1½ inches square, for an overall finished Four Patch size of 3 inches square, start by cutting 2-inch-square patches.

2

A basic Four Patch is easy; it's not complex or innovative on its own. **To dress it up a little, use small Four Patch blocks as units in a larger Four Patch block.** Use your finished 3-inch Four Patches from Step 1 as two of your four larger patches, and cut two 3½-inch squares for the other two patches. **Place the small Four Patches in opposite corners in the block layout, and you have a more complex block, the Double Four Patch.**

3

By sizing up again, you can get even fancier, making a Triple Four Patch. **Make two of the Double Four Patch blocks as described in Step 2, then cut two plain 6½-inch squares.** Lay out the units so the plain squares are in opposite corners, **and you have a Triple Four Patch block.** You can incorporate more fabrics—and more interest— into your block this way.

Four Patches in Place of One

Replacing plain squares with Four Patch blocks isn't limited to Double and Triple Four Patches. **Use a Four Patch to replace any plain square to add complexity and interest to a block.** Choose fabrics that coordinate or contrast with the fabrics in your block; put a jaunty little Four Patch in the center of an otherwise sedate, traditional pieced block.

Echoes in the Middle

Another way to jazz up a block is to replace a plain center square with a smaller version of the block.

In this 12-inch Sawtooth block, the center square is 6 inches, one-half of the total finished block size. **To fill this space with a 6-inch Sawtooth block, start with the *finished* sizes of the patches in the larger block, and divide by 2. The finished size of the center square should be 3 inches, and the triangle squares should finish at 1½ inches. The unfinished center block should measure 6½ inches.**

Tip

Don't forget to add the seam allowances back on when you convert to smaller or larger sizes! If you need a 3-inch finished square, cut a 3½-inch square.

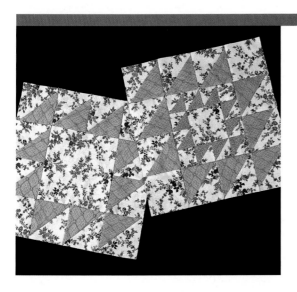

Substituting a pieced block for a plain center gives the block-within-a-block the illusion of depth. It's almost as if you are peering into the center and the pieces are smaller because they are further away from you. Foster this illusion in a medallion-type quilt by starting small and building around the center with the same units in ever-increasing scale.

Tip

Evening Star, Shoo Fly, and Puss in the Corner are three other blocks that lend themselves to nesting a miniature block in the center square.

For a new twist on a sampler quilt, "frame" each of your different pieced blocks with the same larger block pattern, such as the Churn Dash or Monkey Wrench pattern. Start by making the small blocks all the same size. Draft the larger blocks to fit around the small blocks so that the small pieced block replaces what would be a plain center square.

Tip

To do this on a smaller scale, look for commercially printed foundation papers that make miniblock construction quick and easy.

SIMPLY SIZING THINGS UP

Strip Sets:
About Face

Break a few rules and say good-bye to conservative quiltmaking! Award-winning quilter Carol Taylor shares her recipe for successful art quilts. Slice up color-rich strip sets and flip pieces around. Follow her directions, and you'll be amazed at the range of dramatic effects you can produce. Basic piecing skills and an adventurous spirit are all you need to get started.

Getting Ready

A little color theory goes a long way. Look at the 12-section color wheel below. Plan to start your quilt with fabrics in colors that cover half of the color wheel. Begin with one color and follow the color wheel around to choose a sequence of colors that flow together, such as the yellow-to-purple spectrum shown in Step 1 below. You can stick with pure, intense colors, or select a palette of pastels or muted colors. For an accent, find the colors in the middle of your spectrum (reds and oranges, in the photo), then choose colors directly opposite them on the color wheel (blues and greens). Used in smaller amounts, accent colors add a wonderful spark to your quilt.

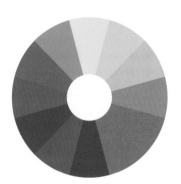

What You'll Need

Fat eighths (9" × 22" pieces) of approximately 25 to 30 fabrics in assorted colors

1 additional yard of a fabric in a color from the middle of your spectrum for alternate strips

1 yard of fabric in an accent color for contrasting strips

Rotary cutting equipment

Sewing machine

Neutral thread

Design wall

Cutting Up a Rainbow

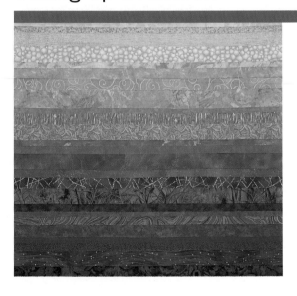

1

Arrange all of your 25 to 30 chosen fabrics in the order that they fall on the color wheel. Cut straight strips from 1 to 4 inches wide and 22 inches long. **Sew the strips together to create a large rainbow strip set.** Press all the seam allowances in the same direction.

Tip

When deciding on colors to use in your quilt, overlap fabric candidates and squint your eyes to see how the colors flow.

2

Cut the strip set into strips perpendicular to your sewn seams. Vary the widths of these cut strips in ½-inch increments, with the narrowest strip no less than 1 inch wide and the widest strip no more than 4 inches wide. Cut on a large cutting mat with a long (24-inch) acrylic ruler. Line up one or more of the lines on your ruler with one or more seams to ensure straight cuts.

Tip

To make cuts longer than your ruler, slide the ruler up, aligning its edge with the last 6 inches of your previous cut.

3

Hang a piece of one of the fabrics used in your strip set on the design wall as a background. **Arrange the strips on top, leaving room between the strips for the background fabric to peek through.** Move the strips around to achieve a balance of wide and narrow strips that looks pleasing to you.

Try the same thing using an accent color as your background. A contrasting fabric may reduce the clamor of the strip sets and unify your design. When you like what you see, cut the background fabric into strips to join to the pieced strips.

Tip

For a quick design wall, hang a piece of flannel or batting, or the wrong side of a vinyl tablecloth, on an empty wall.

4

If there's a color you feel is missing, now is a good time to add it! Add a strip or two of yellow to a dark or drab palette to give it a little spark, or **tone down a too-wild design by introducing a neutral color like black, gray, or tan.**

Tip

For very colorful quilts, strips of a calming, tone-on-tone fabric often work well as blenders without detracting from the design.

Interruptions of color are only one way to shake up the flow of colors across a quilt top. **Another option is to stagger the strips so the colors don't line up.** Move strips in smaller increments to achieve waves, scallops, and zigzags that resemble bargello or flamestitch needlepoint. You might even notice landscapes or cityscapes emerging from such a design! Larger, random increments may produce a powerful abstract design. To end up with an even rectangle, trim the extending strips or add fabric where needed.

Sometimes all it takes to pull a design together is to reverse roles. Keep the strips in roughly the same order as they were in the original top, but **turn every other strip so the spectrum runs in the opposite direction.** This often transforms a previously static design into a seemingly complex pattern with a lot of movement. Set the strips side-by-side, then try the arrangement with the strips spaced out on one of the backgrounds you used in Step 3 on the opposite page. Also, continue to play around with the positioning of narrow and wide strips.

Tip

Try combining a staggered arrangement (as shown in Step 5) with this reversal technique for another design option.

Once you have decided on a design for the center of the quilt, try a few more tricks to see if you can improve on your creation even further. To make your strips appear to "float," **add large, monochromatic strips at the bottom and top, the sides, or both.** Often, plain strips of patterned tone-on-tone fabric can give you just the look you're after. Or, you might piece strips with fabrics in related colors, so that the quilt center is surrounded by a subtle blending of colors that unifies the quilt.

Tip

Don't stop with the first design you like. Snap a Polaroid as a record, then try for something you may like even more.

STRIP SETS: ABOUT FACE

8

Once you find an arrangement you're happy with, take a break from it (preferably overnight), **and then look at it with fresh eyes in the morning.** This way, you'll be sure you're really happy with the design before you piece it together. You may even be struck with a new idea that you hadn't thought of the day before.

9

Tip

Medium gray sewing thread will blend with almost any fabric and not show through.

When you decide on a final design, cut any additional strips necessary, and make sure everything is exactly as you want it on your design wall. Pick up the first two strips and sew them together using a ¼-inch seam allowance. Press the seam allowances to one side, and return the strips to the design wall. Pick up the next two strips and sew them together. Continue, gradually piecing larger sections so you deal with the bulk of the quilt for the least amount of time. **Replace the sections back on the design wall after you sew them, so you keep your design intact.**

10

Tip

Handle bias-cut borders carefully to avoid stretching the edges out of shape before you bind them.

To finish off your new creation, add a border—or two! Since your quilt is already strippy/stripey, **echo that feeling with a strip-pieced border.** Cut varying width strips from matching or accent fabrics, then sew them together into one large, new piece of "striped" fabric. Cut your border strips straight across the seam lines for a more traditional feel, or cut them on the bias for a border that looks a lot more complex than it really is. If the border stripes conflict with the stripes within, add a plain inner border between the quilt top and the pieced border.

The Quilter's
Problem Solver

Too Many Strips

Problem	Solution
I have a stash of strip sets left over from another project. What are some other innovative options for using them?	Cut your strip set into squares or rectangles, then try one of these ideas: ❑ Using random-size squares and rectangles, put them together in an innovative jigsaw set (see page 23). ❑ Surround your cut shapes with Log Cabin–style strips, and set them together in rows (see page 21). ❑ Set squares together, with alternate plain blocks or separated by sashing strips. ❑ Set squares on-point to create new designs.

(see page 23). ... (see page 21).

Skill Builder

Become your own art critic and "virtual designer."

Take a photo (use a Polaroid or digital camera for quick results) of each of the designs you create on your design wall. You'll be able to keep track of your many ideas, and you'll always be able to re-create a design you had before. A photo gives you a more objective view of your design, allowing you to see if there is good structure, balance, and flow. It may also reveal a design flaw you didn't see up close.

Try This!

Recycle abandoned, unfinished quilt tops.

Take out that old quilt top that's been in a drawer because it didn't turn out the way you had hoped. Convince yourself that since you're not excited about completing this project, you have nothing to lose, and an art quilt to gain! Take the risk: Slice it up and put it back together in a whole new way.

You can also use photography to take the risk out of cutting up a quilt top. Take a color Polaroid or regular snapshot of the top and slice up the photo as you would the real thing, but in miniature. Play around with the strips of the photograph until you find a pleasing composition. Then cut and piece the real quilt top in the same design.

STRIP SETS: ABOUT FACE

Adventurous Settings

Perhaps you've amassed a hodgepodge of oddly sized, unrelated orphan blocks from classes, workshops, and your own sewing room experiments. Maybe there is a special fabric you'd like to showcase, or a collection of photos in various sizes you've transferred to fabric. Whatever the circumstances, you know that the typical, traditional, run-of-the-mill set just won't do. Not to worry! Read on for some unusual and creative setting solutions—one of which is sure to fit your needs.

Getting Ready

How you plan your innovative set depends upon what you're starting out with in the way of blocks; it also depends on your quilting personality. If you prefer to have it all on paper before touching fabric, measure and label each of your blocks. Read through this chapter, select an intriguing option, and sketch it on graph paper. Use the sketch as your road map to construct the quilt. Position your blocks and setting pieces on a design wall, and stay open to rearrangements that will strengthen the overall look of the quilt.

If you are the daring kind of person who's willing to fly without a safety net, skip the graph paper and proceed directly to your design wall. Play with various block arrangements, leaving spaces for strips and sashes. Then design the quilt "in the cloth" as you go.

Log Cabin Sets

Perhaps you're starting with blocks of widely varying sizes, and maybe even different shapes. These can be adjusted to a uniform finished size simply by adding strips, Log Cabin–style.

Study the detail of the quilt on the opposite page. Notice that the strips, or logs, vary in width within a single block, and from block to block. They may be added to one, two, or any number of the block's sides. The more variety, the better!

Tip

Feature a special hand-dyed or theme fabric by cutting it into shapes and framing it Log Cabin–style.

2

Select a variety of fabrics for the Log Cabin setting strips. **Use your rotary cutter and acrylic ruler to cut at least one strip from each selected fabric, cutting along either the lengthwise or crosswise grain.** Vary the strip widths from approximately 1 to 4 inches.

Measure each block, and order them from smallest to largest. **Begin with the smallest block, and decide how you will frame it.** For added interest, frame each block in a different way, adding logs to only two sides of one block, to all sides of another, and using alternately wide and narrow strips in a third.

Tip

Place each framed block on a design wall, to make sure logs of the same fabric don't end up next to each other.

3

Tip

Use the wider strips to enlarge the smallest blocks, and save the narrower strips for larger blocks that need less enlarging.

For the first log, cut a strip slightly longer than the edge of the block you will frame. Place the log on the block, with right sides together and long raw edges even. Pin, **then sew the log to the block with a ¼-inch seam allowance.** Press toward the log, and trim the short raw edges even with the block. To keep the lines of the block straight, **use your rotary cutter to square up the block after each addition.** Add strips of different fabrics and widths until the block is at least 3 inches larger than the largest block.

4

Tip

Black-and-white prints make great choices for setting strips when you're combining bright, multi-color scrappy blocks.

When you're done, measure the block. Round the measurement down to the nearest ¼ inch; this number becomes the "target measurement" for all the blocks in the quilt. Working from the next smallest to the largest, follow Steps 2 and 3 to enlarge each block. Add strips in any order, to as many sides as you choose. Square up each block to the target measurement.

Use your design wall to arrange the blocks in straight or diagonal rows, or in any other pleasing arrangement. Sew the blocks together to finish the quilt top, adding borders as desired.

Consider other variations on the Log Cabin setting. In "Photo Fun," Jan Eggleston framed each photo transfer with one round of logs, then cut the logs at an angle. Following a second round of logs, the block was squared up.

This quilt also shows how to combine blocks of different sizes *without* framing them to the same size. Arrange blocks of the same width in vertical rows, ignoring their lengths. An irregular bottom edge adds interest and excitement. Try the same thing with horizontal rows!

See page 25 for an easy way to finish a quilt with irregular edges.

Jigsaw Sets

The focus of a creative set doesn't need to be a block or photo transfer. A special theme fabric that you love can be cut apart and used as the focus for an innovative jigsaw set. Likewise, a variety of similarly themed fabrics can be combined in a single quilt. Examine the theme fabric and select the motifs you wish to feature in your quilt. **Cut squares or rectangles that include the entire desired motif, plus room around them for seam allowances.** There's no need to make the dimensions of these "blocks" uniform.

Fabric companies come out with new theme fabrics every season. Keep an eye out for new favorites.

Play with the cut pieces on your design wall until you find a satisfying arrangement. Don't worry about creating neat rows; just concentrate on pleasing your eye. When you are happy with an arrangement, choose fabrics to coordinate with your

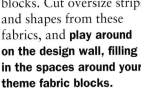

blocks. Cut oversize strips and shapes from these fabrics, and **play around on the design wall, filling in the spaces around your theme fabric blocks.**

23

3

Study your arrangement, and note where you might incorporate Log Cabin–style strips or sashes, or filler strips. Identify larger units that can be assembled with straight seams. If you wish, adjust the layout, or the strips and sashes, to simplify assembly. When you are satisfied with your design, sew the pieces together in sections. **You may find that you are left with a situation that calls for a set-in seam—edges that must fit together and turn a corner.** In the case shown here, the upper right section forms the outside corner, and the L-shaped middle section forms an inside corner.

4

To set in the outside corner, place the L-shaped section right side up, then align the raw edge of the inset section right side down on the left side. Pin and sew with a ¼-inch seam, beginning at the upper edge and working toward the corner. Stop sewing ¼ inch from the edge, and backstitch to secure. **Remove your work from the machine.** Rotate your work; align and pin the adjacent edges together. Again, begin at the outside edge, and sew, stopping ¼ inch from the corner; backstitch two or three stitches to secure. **The stitches should almost touch where the previous line of stitching ended.**

5

Tip

Create strip sets, and rotary cut across the seam allowances to create strips for pieced sashing.

For all set-in seams, press the seam allowances toward the inside corner section, **so the corner is sharp and as flat as the rest of the pieced top.** Once you get used to making set-in seams, you won't go out of your way to avoid them. **As in Susan Else's quilt, Captured on Film, let the overall design dictate the quilt assembly.** A quilt like this is hardly quick or easy. However, the time and patient attention to detail you expend are bound to result in a quilt that will capture the attention and awe of the viewer.

The Quilter's
Problem Solver

Finishing Uneven Edges

Problem

The set you've designed results in a quilt top with irregular edges.

Solution

You can bind your quilt in the usual way; there will simply be more corners to miter. An easier alternative is an envelope finish. With this method, you finish the edges before you quilt.

1. Cut the backing and batting approximately 4 inches larger than the quilt top at its widest vertical and horizontal measurements.
2. Lay out the batting, then center the backing right side up on top. Baste. Center the quilt top *wrong side up* on top, pin to secure, then baste again. Remove the pins.
3. Use a walking foot or even-feed foot. Begin with a few backstitches at the midpoint of one straight section. Stitch a scant ¼ inch from the raw edge of the quilt top, sewing through all three layers. Work your way around the top, pivoting at each angle with the needle down. Finish with a few backstitches, leaving an unsewn 10- to 12-inch opening.
4. Trim the batting and backing even with the quilt top. Trim the batting very close to the stitching line at the quilt top opening, and along angles. Trim the seam allowance at outer corners by clipping across the corner, taking care not to cut the stitching line. Create sharp inner corners by clipping into the seam allowance and eliminating bulk by trimming the seam allowances close to the stitching line.

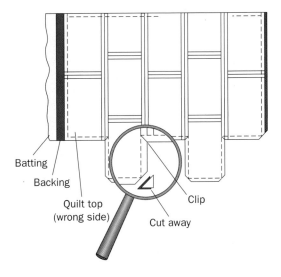

Batting
Backing
Quilt top
(wrong side)
Cut away
Clip

5. Remove the basting. Turn the quilt right side out by pulling it through the opening. Pull out the corners with a needle or pin. At the opening, turn the raw edge of the backing ¼ inch to the inside, covering the edge of the batting. Turn the raw edge of the quilt top to the inside, even with the backing edge. Sew the opening closed by hand, using a blind stitch.
6. Baste, and quilt your quilt as desired.

ADVENTUROUS SETTINGS

Off-Kilter
but On-Target

E ver feel like you just can't follow the rules one more minute, or make the very same block one more time? The cure is at hand. Indulge in a little rebellion, and play around with patterns that are all askew. Make one, make 'em all, or make your own departures from conformity! Throw caution to the wind, but keep your sense of humor and fun close at hand.

Getting Ready

First, pick a traditional block that you'll redesign using this off-kilter or skewed technique. Look through books or magazines for traditional blocks that may adapt well to being redrafted. (Simple blocks with few intersections work best.) Study your chosen block for straight lines that can be angled or moved off center.

While you're not limited to just one block design per quilt, remember that you can redesign the same block in countless ways. Play around and discover the different possibilities. Using many variations of one block design will provide enough diversity to keep you interested, and will also provide a unifying factor for your quilt. More than one block design may detract from the whimsical effect.

What You'll Need

Mechanical pencil

¼- or ⅛-inch graph paper

Marker

Tracing paper

Freezer paper

Masking tape

Fabrics

Rotary cutting supplies

Sewing machine

Basic Skewing

1

Using a pencil, draft the traditional version of your chosen block on graph paper. Draw the block at its finished size (without seam allowances). **Darken the lines of your drawing with a marker.**

2

Tape the graph paper drawing to a work surface. Place a sheet of tracing paper over your drawing and tape it in place. **Use a pencil to trace only the square outline of the block onto the tracing paper.**

Use a clear acrylic ruler and a mechanical pencil for straight, even lines. Your finished block will have neat, true, 90-degree outlines, to contain and restrain the wild lines within.

3

Tip

Tilt your ruler only slightly when drawing your skewed block. You don't want the two horizontal lines to cross each other. Ditto for the two vertical lines.

To create a skewed pattern, use the acrylic ruler and mechanical pencil as follows: **Align the ruler with a straight line within the block, and then tilt the ruler slightly off the straight line and draw a new, angled line with the pencil.** Repeat until all of your inner lines are redrafted at angles to the original lines.

Align the ruler so that the ¼-inch line is along the edge of your block. **Draw seam allowance lines around the edges of your new block.**

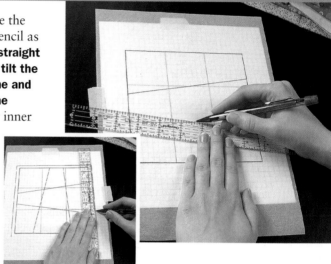

4

Tip

To duplicate a skewed block, stack several layers of tracing paper under your drawing. Stitch along the lines and perforate it using an unthreaded sewing machine.

Examine your drafted off-kilter block to determine the best piecing method. If the block can be divided into sections, try foundation piecing. **Cut your tracing paper drawing into sections for paper-piecing foundations.** Be sure to leave fabric around the edges of the sections for seam allowances.

Here's an alternative to paper piecing: **Cut the tracing paper drawing apart along the seam lines to create finished-size templates for each patch. Use these templates to cut fabric patches for piecing.** Again, add ¼-inch seam allowances along all edges of the templates.

Skewed Nine Patch

Once you begin to play with skewed designs, you'll never want to stop creating them. The Nine Patch lends itself well to this off-kilter technique because it's almost as easy to piece a skewed block as a traditional one. **This traditional Nine Patch block and skewed Nine Patch blocks are all cousins to one another, yet each has its own look.** Use a skewed version whenever you want to add a jolt of animation, movement, or whimsy to your quilt.

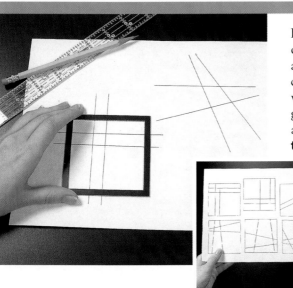

In addition to skewing a Nine Patch design by angling the lines, you can also draft it so the end result is off-center. Draw pairs of horizontal and vertical lines, either parallel or angled. Use a square window template and **move it around on your drawings to audition lots of possibilities.** Draw all the possibilities you like **so you can choose your favorite designs to translate into fabric.**

Tip

Use this skewing technique to create other simple, traditional block patterns based on a four- or nine-patch grid.

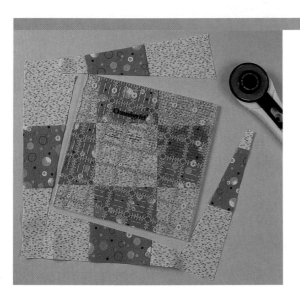

Still another way to skew a block is to **start with an oversize version of a traditional block and then cut it down to produce a smaller block with a skewed design.** A 6½-inch square ruler works well on a 9-inch block. Position the ruler on the block at an angle, and play with various positions to arrive at a design you like. When you're satisfied, rotary cut your skewed 6½-inch block. This block looks best when it's separated from other blocks by sashing or plain alternate blocks.

Tip

Stay stitch around the skewed block so the outside bias edges don't stretch out of shape.

Skewed Log Cabin

1

The traditional Log Cabin block usually begins with a square center patch. From there, rectangular bars surround the center, creating an overlapping look. In the most traditional version, all the "logs" are the same width, and they're all perfect rectangles.

2

For a skewed Log Cabin, redraft all the lines for the logs as described in Steps 1 through 3 on pages 27–28. Vary the width of the logs as much or as little as you want. Log Cabins are easily paper pieced, so you can use your tracing paper drawing as a temporary foundation if you wish.

3

To diverge a little more from the traditional, start with a skewed square as the center of your new block. Or choose a shape with three, five, or six sides to use as your center. Draft your block, using pencil and ruler to add angled lines around the center.

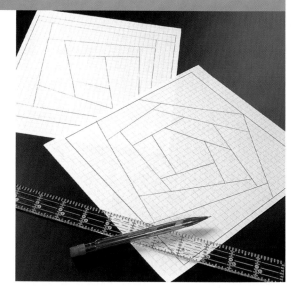

Tip

Grow a rose based on the "Log Cabin" block. Use a five-sided shape for the flower center. Add random-width logs for the petals.

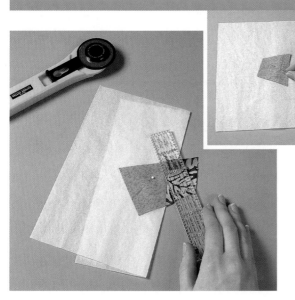

If you're feeling truly adventurous, skip the drafting altogether. Cut a tracing paper foundation the size of your finished block, plus ½ inch for seam allowances. **Pin an odd-shaped patch to the center of your foundation, right side up.** Place a second piece of fabric along an edge of the center patch, right sides together. Sew along the raw edges, then flip open the new log. Fold back the foundation, and **place your rotary ruler so it's at an angle to the seam you just stitched.** Cut along the line to create your skewed log.

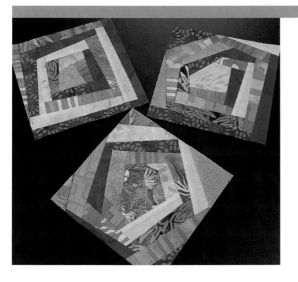

Continue adding logs in this manner around the center patch **until your Log Cabin blocks are complete.** Use a large square rotary ruler to square them up, trimming all the excess fabric from the edges.

Tip

Use a conversation print or a motif from a large-print fabric as the center of your block.

Skewed Flying Geese

For Flying Geese, you'll draft patterns using long strips of freezer paper. This pattern is perfect for long vertical bars, sashing, or borders. Begin by measuring, marking, and cutting out a strip of freezer paper the size of your unfinished unit, including ¼ inch all around for seam allowances. Use a mechanical pencil and acrylic ruler to draw seam lines ¼ inch inside each edge. **Once the side seam lines are drawn, use the ruler to mark dividing lines across the strip. Draw them at different angles, varying the distances between the lines.**

Tip

Freezer paper on a roll is great for designing long borders of Flying Geese. You don't have to tape together sections to achieve the right length!

OFF-KILTER BUT ON-TARGET

31

2

To draw in your Flying Geese, mark an intersection point on every line. This is where the top angles of your triangular Flying Geese will be. Draw a dot anywhere along each line, varying the location from row to row. Stay away from the very edges of the line so that you'll be able to piece the geese easily. Use an acrylic ruler and pencil to **draw connecting lines from the corners of the line below up to the marked dot, forming your skewed Flying Geese.**

3

These Flying Geese are best pieced on a foundation. Begin with the goose triangle on the very bottom, add the background triangles, and then proceed to the next goose. **Continue until your strip is completely pieced.** Each of your geese will seem to have a mind of its own!

Skewed Sawtooth Star

1

To make a slightly askew Sawtooth Star, draw the block on graph paper. Use tracing paper to redraw the block. **Keep the center square and basic grid intact, but skew the triangles on each side.** Mark an off-center dot along each side of the center square. Draw lines from each dot to the outer edges of the block. Cut this pattern into three sections and foundation piece the units. Join the units. When set next to each other, the star points will still meet, just as for traditional Sawtooth Star blocks.

 2

For a star that's even more whimsical and fun, abandon the square center. **Angle the lines of this block just as you did for the Nine Patch in Step 3 on page 28, and then add the star points.** You'll have a background triangle like the Flying Geese pattern (shown on page 31) at the center of each side. The star tips will point every which way for a much more irregular and free-wheeling eight-pointed star. You'll probably find it best to separate blocks of this type with sashing or plain alternate blocks.

Skewed Heart

1

To make a pieced Heart block, start with a standard, curved design. Fold a piece of paper to the size of your desired finished block. Mark and cut out a half heart, and unfold it to complete the pattern. Trace the heart onto a square block. Straighten out the curved lines to make a simple, easy-to-piece design. The fold line of the pattern represents the "axis" on which this design is built. **To skew the design, move the axis off center, or angle the axis.** Part of the charm of a skewed design is its asymmetry.

2

Assemble a quilt using many variations of just one skewed block design. Try adding a few blocks that are one-quarter the size of the others. Piece these blocks in groups of four, and scatter them randomly throughout the quilt top in place of one large block. Add to the sense of fun with your choice of fabrics: bright, complementary colors and jazzy prints. Or, use your preferred color palette; skewed designs can be just as interesting when made with subtle color gradations, solids, or even traditional quilting prints.

Tip

Refer to "Simply Sizing Things Up" on page 10, and adapt those ideas to skewed blocks.

OFF-KILTER BUT ON-TARGET

From Rectangles
to Stars

There may not be an easier way than this to scatter stars across the top of your next quilt. All you do is sew a small rectangle to a larger rectangle to create one unit. Four units create a four-pointed star. This is the perfect way to feature your favorite fabrics. The technique is so quick and simple that you'll be able to make a bed-size version and be snuggling under the stars by the next new moon.

Getting Ready

First, decide what size rectangular unit you would like to work with (this is the size you will cut your background rectangles). For a smaller wallhanging, you'll want smaller units, and our samples, at 4 × 6 inches, are a good size. If you're planning on making a larger lap or bed quilt, use larger, 6 × 8-inch units to make your construction go quicker and to keep the proportions in scale.

When choosing fabrics, first plan out your background values and colors. Arrange fabrics on your design wall, and move them around until you have a pleasing flow of color and value. Then, decide where you want stars to appear, and choose a fabric for each star that has high contrast with each of its four background fabrics. You'll cut the star fabrics into smaller rectangles, which you will then sew onto the background rectangles to make the star point units.

Making Star Points

Once you have chosen your fabrics and decided on a background rectangle size, you are ready to cut your rectangles. You'll need large background rectangles and small star point rectangles. Cut your background rectangles to the desired size, plus ½ inch for seam allowances. The blocks shown here feature 4 × 6-inch finished-size units, so the background rectangles are cut to 4½ × 6½ inches. **Arrange these background rectangles on your design wall.** Choose various intersections of four background rectangles where you will place a star.

Tip

Pin a scrap of star fabric at each intersection where you plan to place a star.

2

Calculate the size of the star point rectangles. You'll need two long and two short rectangles for each star.

The finished length of each star point is 1 inch less than the background rectangle. Here, it's 6 – 1 = 5 inches for the long side, and 4 – 1 = 3 inches for the short side. Add ½ inch for seam allowances; cut the long point rectangles 5½ inches long and the short point rectangles 3½ inches long.

The star points' width is one-fourth the background rectangles' width. Here, it's 4 × .25 = 1 inch. Add ½ inch for seam allowances, and cut each star point rectangle 1½ inches wide.

3

To position a long star point rectangle on the background rectangle, you'll need to mark placement lines. On the *wrong* side of your long star point rectangle, **use a pencil to draw a mark at each end of one long side, ¼ inch in from the raw edge.**

Mark a placement line for the star point rectangle on the *right* side of the background rectangle. **Measure in along a short edge a distance equal to the finished width of the star point rectangle, plus ¼ inch, and make a mark.** (In our example, this distance is 1¼ inches.)

4

Place the long star point rectangle on the background rectangle, right sides together. **Match the marked seam allowance at one end of the star point with your mark on the background. Rotate the other end of the star point until its seam allowance mark aligns with the raw edge of the background.**

Pin the star point to the background, and sew ¼ inch inside the marked long edge of the star point. Press the star point out. Place the unit right side down on a cutting mat, align a ruler with the raw edges of the background, and **trim the edges of the star point even with the background.**

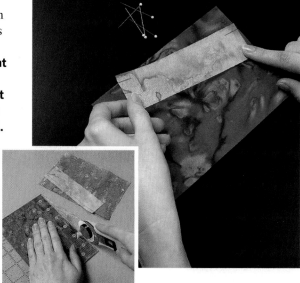

To position a short star point rectangle on the background rectangle, mark the ¼-inch seam allowance on the *wrong* side of your star point, and the placement of the star point rectangle on the *right* side of the background, as you did in Step 3 on the opposite page. For the background's placement mark, measure in along a *long* edge 1¼ inches.

Position, sew, press, and **trim the star point** as you did in Step 4 on the opposite page.

Tip

To help you remember where to mark: For long star points, measure in along a short side; for short star points, measure in along a long side.

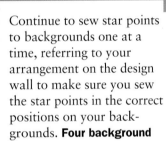

Continue to sew star points to backgrounds one at a time, referring to your arrangement on the design wall to make sure you sew the star points in the correct positions on your backgrounds. **Four background rectangles, two with long points and two with short points, make a complete star.**

Sew the background rectangles together into rows, pressing the seam allowances in opposite directions from row to row. **Sew the rows together to complete your quilt top.**

Adding Borders

This quilt really sparkles with a snappy narrow (¾- to 1½-inch) inner border that echoes the narrowness of the star points. Consider the inner border the "zinger"—use a fabric, value, or color that has not been used in the quilt. **Audition a bold stripe or a fabric in a color that has good contrast with the rest of the quilt.**

Once you've added an inner border, add a wider outer border. For proportion and balance, keep each border strip no wider than a background rectangle. Bind your quilt with the same, outer border fabric.

Tip

After quilting and binding, add a little extra starshine! Embellish the center of each star with luminescent glass beads.

A New Look from
Attic Windows

Most quilters know the traditional Attic Windows design, a square or rectangle framed by sashes that give the illusion of looking through a window. The three-dimensional look of this block takes on a whole new perspective when the window setting is changed to a diamond and the design gets a new "slant." Enjoy the view!

Getting Ready

Before starting on this new Attic Windows block, do a little prep work that will make your quiltmaking easier. Make sure your sewing machine is set up to easily produce accurate ¼-inch seam allowances. Because Attic Windows requires a light fabric, a dark fabric, and a medium fabric to achieve the illusion of depth, a value finder is also helpful. This red transparent plastic viewer makes all of your fabrics look red, allowing you to focus only on their relative lightness or darkness. Value finders are available at quilt shops or from mail order sources. In addition, try a full-spectrum lightbulb if you don't have good natural lighting in your sewing area. It will simulate natural light and help you pick the right fabrics for your blocks.

The Attic Windows blocks shown here feature 3½-inch-wide 60-degree diamonds. If you wish to make larger or smaller ones, adjust the length of the sashes (window frames) to match the edges of the diamonds you use and keep the sashing width in proportion.

Piecing the Units

Attic Windows is a traditional quilt pattern that suggests some visual depth, achieved by the mitered angle of the "window frame" sashing. The fabric of the "window" area is often patterned for visual interest.

Traditional Attic Windows blocks are square or rectangular. **However, this design takes a new look at the traditional block and puts a slant on it, using diamonds to create more visual depth.**

2

For the windows, select a medium-value fabric. It is most effective to use only one fabric for all the windows within a quilt. Hand-painted fabrics are especially striking, since they offer subtle color changes within one single piece of fabric. Next, select a light and a dark sashing fabric. **Choose colors that complement your window fabric without blending with it;** you need a high degree of contrast to get the three-dimensional effect.

Tip

Before cutting, apply spray sizing to the fabric and iron it. The sizing will help prevent the bias edges of the patches from stretching.

3

For the window diamonds, cut a 3½-inch strip from your medium-value fabric. **Position an acrylic ruler on the strip so that the 60-degree angle line is along the bottom edge of the strip (the ruler will lean to the left).** Cut along the ruler's edge and discard the trimmed-off piece.

Rotate your mat so the newly angled edge is to your left. **Position the ruler so that the 3½-inch line aligns with the newly cut edge and the 60-degree angle line aligns with the bottom edge of the strip. Cut along the edge of the ruler.** Repeat to cut as many diamonds as you need.

4

Tip

To make cutting small pieces easier, use your smallest ruler that has a 60-degree line.

To cut sashes, cut 1½-inch strips from your light and dark fabrics. Cut these into 1½ × 5½-inch rectangles. Position the ruler on the strip so the 60-degree angle line is along the bottom edge of the strip (the ruler will lean to the left). Line up the edge of the ruler with the bottom right corner of the rectangle. **Trim away the corner of the rectangle.**

Rotate the mat so the newly angled edge is to your left. **Align the other 60-degree angle line with the bottom, aligning the edge of the ruler with the top right corner. Trim away; discard the corners.**

Use a ruler and a mechanical pencil to find the intersection of the ¼-inch seam allowances on the wrong side of the diamond at the obtuse angle. **Mark a dot exactly where the seam allowances intersect.** Place a light sashing piece consistently on the same side of the diamond, with right sides together and the edges even at the obtuse angle. Sew with the diamond on top, beginning at the dot. Sew one stitch, backstitch one stitch, **then sew to the opposite edge.**

Repeat Step 5, this time marking the dot on the dark sash, which will be on top as you sew. Fold the light sash out of the way and **sew from the dot to the opposite edge.**

Bring the adjoining edges of the light and dark sashes together, and align the short raw edges. Beginning just outside the dot on the dark sash, take one stitch, backstitch once, then sew to the edge, completing the window unit. **Press all seams away from the diamond.**

Tip

On dark fabrics, use a white fabric marker; a Nonce pencil leaves a lasting mark that's easily removed with a damp cloth.

Completing the Quilt Top

Place your window units on a design wall or other surface, arranging them in rows. Because of the construction process, you will have jagged edges and windows along the edges that are missing sashes. Before you sew the windows into rows, **add any additional outer sashes, cut to the same size as before, to completely surround each window as needed.** Sew them on as you did in Steps 5 and 6 above.

2

To straighten the edges so you end up with a squared-up quilt, you could simply cut off the ragged edges with a rotary cutter and acrylic ruler. Or, you can fill in the outer angled spaces with triangles cut from the fabrics you used to make the quilt. To do this, **refer to the labels on the photograph** and to your quilt, and cut the shapes as described below.

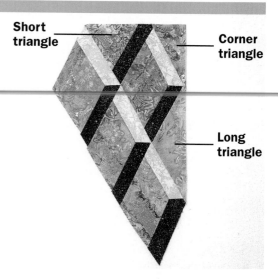

Short triangle

Corner triangle

Long triangle

Tip

Corner triangles go in the corners, short triangles go along the top and bottom edges, and long triangles go on the sides.

Short triangle: Cut a 3¾-inch strip. Cut diamonds as directed in Step 3 on page 40, using the 60-degree angle line and the 3¾-inch line. Cut this diamond in half to make two short triangles.

Long triangle: Cut a 2¾-inch strip; cut the strip into 9⅛-inch rectangles. Lay the 30-degree angle line along the bottom of the rectangle and align the edge of the ruler with the bottom corner. Cut off the edge; repeat on the other end to make a long triangle.

Corner triangle: Cut a 2¾-inch strip; cut the strip into 4¾-inch rectangles. Cut the rectangle in half diagonally to make two corner triangles.

3

On the design wall, separate the sashed windows into diagonal rows. **Add the short, long, and corner triangles to fill in the outside edges of your layout.** Sew the triangle pieces and the window units into these rows, then sew the rows together. Add a border if you like, or simply use a narrow binding to contain the design.

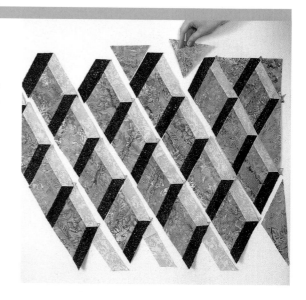

The Quilter's
Problem Solver

Refining the Finished Product

Problem	Solution
I want to add a border without squaring up the quilt with side triangles. How do I do this?	Instead of adding the outer triangles to square out the design, appliqué the quilt top onto a border.
My Attic Windows layout on the design wall does not have depth.	You need more contrast in your sashes. The design will run together if the sashes are not very light and very dark. Also, avoid busy prints in the sashes; quiet patterns or tone-on-tone fabrics work best.

Skill Builder

It's all in the details.

When sewing, the proper needle and thread can make all the difference. Needle manufacturers recommend you change your needle after every 8 to 10 hours of sewing. Many quilters prefer to use a 10/75 jeans needle for machine piecing. It is a finer, sharper needle, and it leaves a smaller hole in the fabric. However, it is more fragile, so avoid sewing over pins with this needle.

To avoid frequently changing thread colors, use a neutral thread such as off-white, beige, or light gray. Neutral thread will work with every color fabric, even dark fabric. For best results, use a good-quality thread in both the top of the machine and the bobbin.

For a fine seam, use 100 percent mercerized cotton thread made of long Egyptian cotton such as Madeira Tanne 50 wt.

Try This!

Personalize your Attic Windows.

Choose a themed fabric for the window portion of your quilt.

❑ Use animal prints for an animal lover.

❑ Pick a whimsical juvenile print for a child's room.

❑ Choose a hunting or fishing print for your favorite outdoorsman.

❑ Look for a floral or gardening-design print for the gardening enthusiast.

Show-Stopping
Pieced Appliqué

Combining piecing with appliqué can produce some pretty luscious effects. As you break up motifs into patches, you add visual depth. Even the simplest shapes will appear much more complex as a result. Despite the "berry" easy piecing, this technique will have viewers wondering, "How did she do that?"

Getting Ready

Choose a design that you'd like to appliqué. Sketch your own design, or look for inspiration in children's coloring books; many of them have fun, imaginative drawings that translate well to appliqué. Since you'll be piecing your design first and eventually appliquéing it to a background, choose a simple, unfussy shape with smooth edges and mostly gentle curves along the outer edge. The larger it is, the more piecing you can include.

This technique uses freezer paper as a tool to create the pieced appliqué. It works well because it's somewhat translucent, so you can xeasily trace your design. Also, the wax coating "holds" your fabric in place when pressed with an iron, so you don't have to contend with slipping fabric.

What You'll Need

Appliqué pattern or sketch

Freezer paper

Masking tape

100% cotton fabrics

Fine-tip permanent marker

Paper scissors

Fabric scissors

Sewing machine

Open-toe presser foot (optional)

Thread

Thread snips

Quilters' GluTube (or other temporary-hold fabric adhesive)

Temporary stabilizer

Making Your Pieced Appliqués

1

Draw or trace your design on paper, including all the features you wish to include in your final pieced appliqué. It may be necessary to divide your design into two or more sections to facilitate piecing. Within each section, divide the space into roughly rectangular segments, using a ruler to mark straight lines that completely cross a section from side to side. If you choose to sketch in pencil, go over the final lines with a marker.

2

Tape the paper drawing to your work surface. Tape a piece of freezer paper, shiny side down, on top of your drawing. **Using a fine-tip permanent marker, trace your design onto the freezer paper,** transferring all the lines that you will use in piecing your appliqué. Use a pair of sharp paper scissors to **cut out your entire freezer paper pattern along the outer drawn edge of the pieced appliqué shape.**

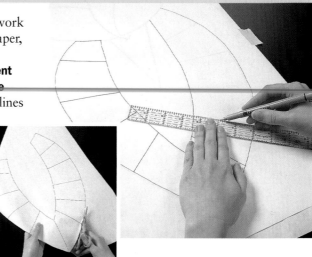

3

Choose fabrics to use for piecing your appliqué. For the look of subtle shading, piece each section of the appliqué with colors in the same value range, but with different visual textures. For example, the fabrics in the strawberry appliqué are all reds, but they vary slightly in tone, scale, and pattern, giving the patchwork combination visual interest.

Arrange your fabrics in various groupings until you are pleased with the order. Snip a small piece of each fabric and **glue it to the appropriate segment on your original drawing** to use as a guide for fabric placement.

4

Cut a piece of fabric large enough to cover the first segment of the appliqué piece, plus a ¼-inch seam allowance on all sides. (When in doubt, cut larger. It's better to have too much fabric and trim than to have too little fabric and have to rip out a seam and start over.) **Place the wrong side of the fabric against the shiny, coated side of the freezer paper pattern so that it completely covers the first segment.** Hold the piece up to the light so you can see through to check for adequate coverage. Iron to bond the fabric in place, pressing on the uncoated freezer paper side *only* where it overlaps fabric.

Cut another piece of fabric large enough to completely cover the next segment, plus seam allowances. Place it on top of the first piece of fabric, right sides together. Angle the piece so that it will lie across the pattern correctly when flipped. **To double-check your placement, flip it out along where you'll sew your seam and check that it actually covers the next segment.**

Set your machine for a short stitch length (14 to 16 stitches per inch) when sewing through paper. The short stitches will perforate the paper, making it easier to remove it later. Pin the fabric in place, then turn the freezer paper pattern over and **sew on the marked line separating the first and second segments.** Sew from raw edge to raw edge of the fabric pieces.

Tip

On European machines, a setting of 1.5 will give you approximately 14 to 16 stitches per inch.

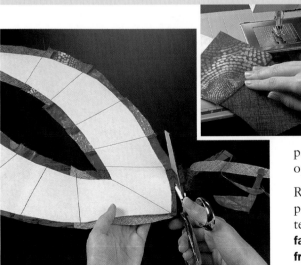

Use scissors to trim the seam allowances of the seam you just sewed to approximately ¼ inch. **Open out the second piece of fabric and gently finger press the seam.** Press the fabric to the freezer paper pattern as you did in Step 4 on the opposite page.

Repeat this "sew, trim, flip, and press" procedure until the entire pattern is covered with fabric. **Trim fabric that extends beyond the freezer paper pattern to ¼ inch, for seam allowances.**

SHOW-STOPPING PIECED APPLIQUÉ

8

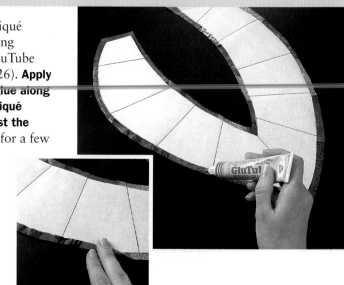

For help turning under appliqué edges, use a temporary basting product such as Quilters' GluTube (see "Resources" on page 126). **Apply a light, continuous bead of glue along the edge of your pieced appliqué where the fabric extends past the pattern.** Let the glue air-dry for a few seconds, then gently fold the edges in along the edge of the freezer paper pattern and press them down. **Smooth the edges as you go, using your fingers to ease in fullness and coax curves to lie flat.**

Tip

Apply glue to only a few inches at a time; peel and reposition the fabric if necessary to create a smooth edge.

9

Allow the glue to dry for at least 20 minutes. If you will be using machine appliqué, place a layer of temporary stabilizer underneath the background fabric. Pellon Stitch-n-Tear is a good choice, especially if you're using decorative stitching to secure your appliqué to the background. (You'll tear away the stabilizer once the appliqués are sewn on securely.) **Position the finished appliqué on your background fabric and secure through all layers with pins or Quilters' GluTube.**

Tip

A pieced background is a fun way to set off your pieced appliqué. Just make sure it doesn't overwhelm your designs.

10

Stitch the appliqué to the background by hand or machine, using your favorite method. For a speedy appliqué technique, use clear monofilament thread in your machine and cotton in the bobbin, and sew the edges with a blind hem stitch to attach your appliqué "invisibly."

After all your appliqués are sewn to the background, tear away the stabilizer. Trim the background fabric from behind each appliqué and remove the freezer paper.

Tip

Attach your appliqué and embellish the seams between pieces with decorative stitches and special threads.

The Quilter's
Problem Solver

Edgy Solutions

Problem	Solution
Your seam allowance around the outside of your pieced appliqué isn't wide enough to turn under and stitch.	Don't worry! Simply apply paper-backed fusible web to the wrong side, trim the fused appliqué and the fusible web to the exact finished size, and fuse it to the background. Satin stitch around the edges to secure the appliqué to the background fabric.
Your appliqué design gets lost on the background.	Outline the shapes dramatically with decorative threads. Choose a thick, textured, or fuzzy decorative thread, lay it along the edge of your appliqué shape, and couch it in place with a zigzag stitch.

Skill Builder

Develop an eye for choosing and combining fabrics for each pieced appliqué.

Too much variety in color or value within the shape will make it look choppy and disjointed. Stay within the same color family and keep to similar values (the relative lightness or darkness of the color). However, vary the type of printed or woven patterns, the scale, and the direction of the fabric pattern to give your design a sense of liveliness. Start with your stash at home, then head to your local quilt shop to fill in the gaps.

Try This!

Set off pieced appliqués on a coordinating pieced background.

Use fabrics that blend together easily so that your eye is drawn to your appliqués and not distracted by a too-busy background. You can piece your background randomly, strip-piece it, or use a combination of techniques to construct it. Or, use gradated fabrics for a background that's subtly shaded from one side to the other.

Easy Pieced
Landscapes

I f you've been longing to make a landscape quilt, but you don't know where to begin, this chapter is for you. Try this liberating strip-piecing technique for quick and effective landscape backgrounds. And once you've constructed your scenery, you can add appliquéd or embellished details. Just think of it as painting with fabric...and imagine the fun you'll have collecting materials to fill your "paintbox!"

Getting Ready

With this technique, simple landscape backgrounds are assembled in strip-pieced panels. Panels can vary in width and length to fit the design of your quilt, and the fabrics you choose create a striated palette for you to add details onto.

First, decide what type of landscape you'd like to create. Pick fabrics in the colors that will portray your setting best: blues and greens for gentle seascapes, tans and browns for sunbaked desert scenes. Subtle tone-on-tone patterns, large-scale motifs, hand-dyes, batiks, abstracts, and nature prints blend well without disturbing the flow of your design. Decide on the size of your panels, then gather your fabrics and any other inspiration you may want, such as photographs, magazines, or art reproductions. This will help you as you plan out your landscape background. Include the entire "family" of each color, spanning a broad range of values from light to dark.

Creating Your Landscape

1

Use colored pencils or crayons to sketch your landscape, including the basic colors you plan to use. Play with the placement of your colors, and make sure the colors flow nicely from one to the next. Consider both blending from color to color and shading from light to dark, depending on the landscape you plan to portray. Also, decide on whether your predominating seam lines will run horizontally or vertically, or whether they'll radiate out from a corner.

2

Depending on the sizes of your fabric pieces, you may want to break your drawing up into smaller panels. If you are working with fat quarters, for example, a panel should be no more than 18 inches wide.

Divide your drawing into panels as desired, and **arrange the fabrics in order to match your drawing.** Mark or color in your drawing with the specific colors, fabrics, or textures you will use to make the panels. Each panel will be made of several strips of varying widths and angles.

3

Pick up two fabrics from one end of your arrangement. Place them right sides together with the lighter fabric on top, aligning the longest raw edges. This long raw edge should measure a few inches wider than the desired width of the panel.

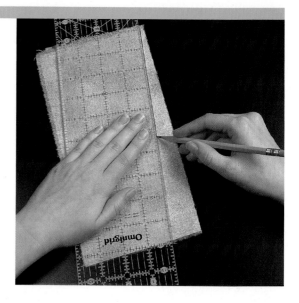

Use a ruler and pencil to mark a line on the top fabric that gently angles away from the long edge. Sew the fabrics together along your drawn line.

4

Tip

Remember: You are working with bias edges, so treat the pieces gently as you cut, sew, and press.

Move to your cutting mat. Place the sewn piece on the mat with the sewn seam to your right (if you are right-handed). Position an acrylic ruler with its ¼-inch line on top of the sewn seam. **Trim away the excess fabric from the sewn seam, leaving ¼-inch seam allowances. Open up the fabrics and press the seam open.**

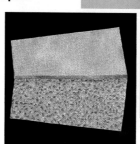

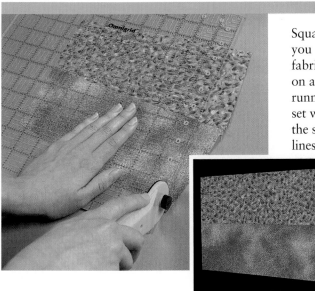

Square up your panel now, so that you have a size guide as you add more fabrics. Place the piece right side up on a cutting mat with the sewn seam running from left to right (for a strip set with horizontal seams). Make sure the seam is at a slight angle to the lines running horizontally on your ruler so that your seam will be at an angle in the finished panel. **Use a rotary cutter and ruler to straighten the panel's side edges, trimming it to the desired width, plus ½ inch for seam allowances.**

Use the rotary cutter and ruler to trim the two long raw edges (the ones that run in the same general direction as your sewn seam) at gentle angles. Make each strip as wide as you like, keeping in mind your drawing and the number of additional fabrics you will be adding to the panel. For the best results, angle the cuts so that the newly cut edges slant in opposite directions from the original angled seam.

Tip

Use the trimmed-off fabric as a strip in another panel.

With right sides together, align the raw edge of the next fabric with an angled raw edge of the panel in progress. Be sure the new piece of fabric is wide enough to extend an inch or two beyond the panel on both sides. **Pin the new fabric in place** and sew, using a ¼-inch seam allowance. Unfold the new strip, press the seam allowances open, and straighten the side edges. **Cut the long edge of the new strip to the desired angle.**

Tip

To create a radiating or fanlike design, angle all your lines in the same direction.

E A S Y   P I E C E D   L A N D S C A P E S

Tip

A large square acrylic ruler is helpful when you're squaring-up panels.

8

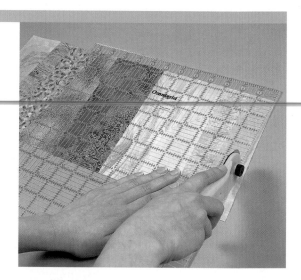

Continue adding fabrics to the panel, as described above. When the panel has reached the desired length, **use a rotary cutter and acrylic ruler to** cut the top and bottom fabrics perpendicular to the sides of the panel, so that the edges and corners of your piece are straight and square.

9

Carefully press the panel from both the back and the front. For added stability, spray the right side with starch or fabric sizing as you press.

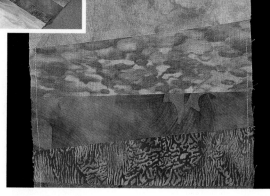

To prevent stretching and raveling of the bias edges, stabilize the completed panels further by **stay-stitching a scant ¼ inch from the raw edges all around the perimeter of the panel.**

10

Tip

Don't worry about matching seams when sewing one panel to another. The mismatched seams and opposing angles add interest and realism to the landscape.

Construct the desired number of panels to serve as the background for your landscape. **With right sides together and edges aligned, pin the panels together,** then sew, using ¼-inch seam allowances. Press the seam allowances to one side.

Square up the entire background, adding stay stitching along raw edges if needed. Add borders or embellishments as desired (see "Skill Builder" on the opposite page).

The Quilter's
Problem Solver

Adding Dimension

Problem	Solution
You want to create the illusion of depth and perspective in your two-dimensional fabric landscape.	Try one of these easy ways to trick the eye: ❏ Vary the width of the strips as you construct each panel. Keep the narrowest strips at the top of the panel, gradually increasing their width as you work your way to the bottom of the panel. Narrow strips appear more distant, while wider strips seem closer, creating a foreground for the scene. ❏ Use the lightest, palest, most indistinct and muted fabrics for the areas you wish to appear furthest away. Save the darkest, brightest, and most detailed fabrics for the foreground. ❏ Position pieced, appliquéd, or fused details, as well as any embellishments, to your advantage. Small-scale, subtly colored additions will appear more distant, while larger, more intensely colored details seem closer to the eye.

Skill Builder

Use nontraditional fabrics, embellishments, and surface design to personalize your landscape.

Satins, silks, and velvets reflect light differently, and can easily mimic water, sky, or snow. An overlay of netting or tulle suggests mist, fog, frost, or smoke. Appliqués, whether your own or purchased, are great for introducing detail. They can be stitched by hand or machine, or they can be fused. Create special effects with buttons, beads, charms, decorative threads, ribbons and trims, fabric paint, markers, and rubber stamps. Your only limit is your imagination!

Try This!

Make beach umbrellas by piecing striped fabric.

Notice the umbrellas in the quilt on page 50, enhancing the landscape? This design of concentric hexagons is easy to do. Use a 60-degree triangle template to cut six "pie wedge" patches from a striped fabric. Use tape on the ruler to help you position the stripes identically on each wedge. Sew them into a hexagon, matching the stripes along each seam. Appliqué the finished, kaleidoscopic shape onto your landscape. You can use striped fabric in similar ways to create pieced appliqués with the illusion of concentric squares or octagons.

Take a Picture, *Make a Quilt*

Have you ever wanted to translate a favorite photo into a quilt? Have you seen realistic-looking quilts hanging in shows and wondered how they're done? Picture a sentimental view of your home, a favorite landmark, or a vacation destination in fabric. You can do it! Go from photo to drawing to quilt, with charming results, using Elsie Vredenberg's easy-to-learn technique. With just a little planning, you'll work with simple, straight lines and avoid troublesome set-in seams.

Getting Ready

Select a well-composed photo with simple lines and a minimum of detail. As you become more proficient, you can add details and complexity. If your photo is small, have it enlarged at a photo shop, or do it with your computer and scanner. Keep in mind that the more you enlarge the photo, the "fuzzier" it gets. If you are making a large quilt instead of the single block shown on the following pages, you can go on to enlarge your line drawing, rather than the photo, to the desired size, working in sections as necessary.

Choose fabrics that match the colors and textures in the photo as closely as you wish. So many fabrics now mimic the look of wood grain, water, rocks, skies, and building materials that it's easy to get a realistic-looking texture for almost every feature in your photo. But don't feel you have to limit yourself to realistic prints. Search out overall patterns, such as small-scale plaids, that will also give you the colors, textures, and general effects you're looking for.

What You'll Need

- **Photograph**
- **Fabrics to represent areas in the photo**
- **Masking and clear tapes**
- **Tracing paper**
- **Freezer paper**
- **Sharp pencil**
- **Fine-point permanent markers (2 or more colors)**
- **Photocopier**
- **Colored pencils**
- **Rotary cutting supplies**
- **Large square acrylic ruler**
- **Fabric and paper scissors**
- **Iron and ironing board**
- **Straight pins**
- **Sewing machine**
- **Neutral thread**

Tracing the Photo

1

To decide which portion of the photo you will transform into a quilt, make a two-piece "window frame." Cut two large L-shapes from paper or light cardboard, and use them to help determine whether your quilt will be square or rectangular, and what part of the image will be included. **Move the Ls around in relation to each other until you frame the portion of the photo you want to include in your quilt.** Use masking tape to tape the Ls together. Secure them in position over the photo, taping them to the back so as not to damage the photo.

2

Place a sheet of tracing paper over your framed photo; tape the photo and the paper to your work surface with masking tape. Using a sharp pencil, lightly trace the lines you want to include in your fabric picture. (Don't press so hard that you damage your photograph.) Keep the drawing simple, tracing only main features. **Move the tracing paper as needed to "fudge" the photo a bit.** In this tracing, the lighthouse was brought closer to the foreground to minimize the water. Remove the tracing paper and **darken the lines with a fine-point permanent marker.**

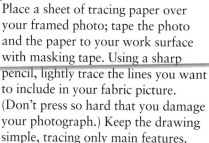

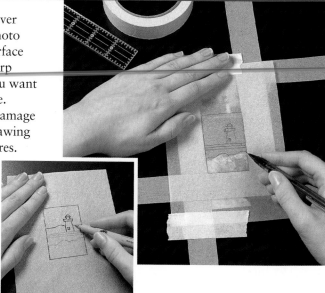

Tip

As you trace, use a ruler to make sure straight lines are straight. Move objects slightly, if necessary, to create a pleasing balance.

3

Enlarge your tracing on a photocopier to the desired finished size of your quilt. Depending on the copier, you will probably have to enlarge your tracing more than once before it is the final size you want. **If the enlargement is too large for a single sheet of copier paper, enlarge your tracing in sections and tape them together with clear tape.**

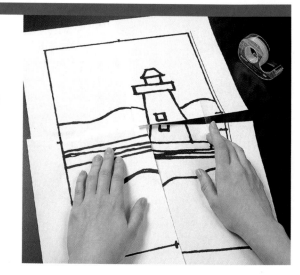

Tip

If you have a computer and scanner with graphic capabilities, you can use them to enlarge your tracing.

4

Use masking tape to tape the enlargement to your work surface, and tape a piece of tracing paper (pieced with clear tape, if necessary) on top. Using a sharp pencil, trace the entire design. To avoid having to sew curved seams, redraw the curves with short, straight lines that preserve the illusion of curves. **Place an acrylic ruler over the curve to trace as long a straight line as you can while staying with the curve.** Move the ruler along the curve, reproducing the curve with straight lines in this manner until the entire curve has been "sectioned."

Tip

Enlarging the original tracing also thickens the drawn lines. When tracing again, follow the center of the line.

Preparing the Master Pattern

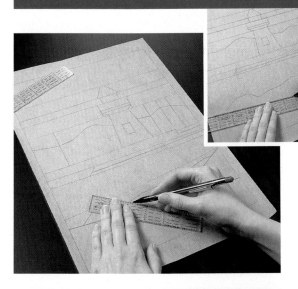

1

Each line you draw will be a sewn seam in your quilt. Identify places where a seam line goes across the whole drawing, then find areas that create straight-lined subdivisions. Use your ruler to find lines that can become part of the same seam line; **draw these lines.** Once you identify and draw in all the major sections, **divide those sections into two or more parts,** always drawing completely across the section.

Tip

Color your design with colored pencils to help you visualize which areas will be pieced from the same fabrics.

2

If one of your sections has a "corner" or an angle that does not extend to an outside edge of that section, add one or more sewing lines so you don't have to set in any pieces. If your angle is somewhat square, like the lighthouse windows in this sketch, **extend one of the angle lines to continue out to an edge.** For sharp or wide angles, cut the angle in half so you can piece the inside and outside angles, then assemble them. **Adding seam lines in consistent patterns, like vertical panels for a background area, will make the piecing less noticeable.**

Tip

Use a pencil to create your master pattern. If you find another way to draw sections that results in larger patches, you can easily erase and redraw your lines.

3

To make a quilt that duplicates, rather than mirrors, your photo, you will need to reverse your drawn design. **Turn your completed tracing paper drawing over, and darken all the lines with a fine-point permanent marker.** Use a bolder line for the major section lines and a different-colored marker for the lines within each smaller section.

TAKE A PICTURE, MAKE A QUILT

59

4

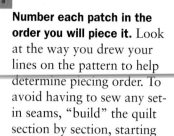

Number each patch in the order you will piece it. Look at the way you drew your lines on the pattern to help determine piecing order. To avoid having to sew any set-in seams, "build" the quilt section by section, starting with two pieces that are sewn together with a single seam, then add to that starting pair one seam at a time.

Choose a letter to represent each fabric you will use. **Label each piece of the pattern with the letter corresponding to the fabric you've chosen for that area.**

5

Tape freezer paper *dull side up* over the pattern. If necessary, overlap pieces of freezer paper and press the overlap with an iron to create a large enough piece. **Using a sharp pencil, trace and transfer all lines, letters, and numbers to the freezer paper** (which will become your templates). If you have trouble seeing through the freezer paper, hold your pattern up to a sunny window, or use a light box to trace it. Keep the original pattern as your master; it will be a handy reference as you piece the picture.

Constructing Your Picture

1

Cut apart the freezer paper copy of the pattern along your drawn lines to make individual templates. Sort the pieces by their fabric letter, so that all the pieces to be pressed onto the same fabric are together. Leave at least ½ inch between the pieces for seam allowances. **With a hot, dry iron, press the shiny side of each freezer paper template onto the wrong side of its corresponding fabric.** Press for a few seconds; if the freezer paper comes loose as you are working, simply press it again.

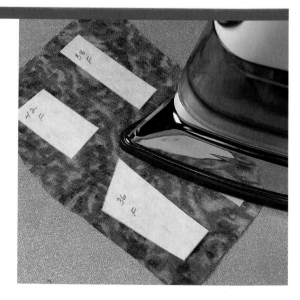

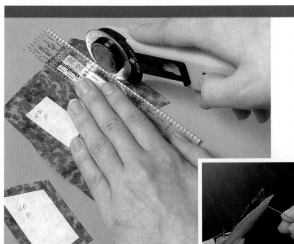

Cut out each patch, using a rotary cutter and acrylic ruler to add ¼-inch seam allowances. Lay out each section's pieces in the numbered order.

Pick up the first two pieces and place them right sides together, aligning the edges to be sewn. Place a pin through the top patch, exactly at the corner of the template, then through the bottom patch, exactly at its corresponding corner. **Repeat at the other end of the edge to be stitched.** For longer patches, insert additional pins in between.

Stitch the pieces together along the edges of the freezer paper. Sew as close to the paper as you can without stitching through it, and remove pins as you come to them. Remove the freezer paper after sewing all edges.

Press the seam allowances toward the piece that appears to be in "front" in the picture. This extra bulk behind an area will make it seem to advance toward the viewer. If you have an area with a lot of seams and the quilt top looks lumpy, press the seams open.

As you complete each seam, compare it to your master pattern to catch mistakes as they occur. Pick up the next numbered piece and sew it on, comparing its position to the pattern. Continue adding pieces in numerical order until each section is complete, then sew the sections together. **Press the quilt on the right side.** Use light steam, and press gently to avoid stretching the fabrics. Use a rotary cutter and large square acrylic ruler to square up the finished piece and trim the edges even.

TAKE A PICTURE, MAKE A QUILT

61

Deep Space
Checkerboards

Awaken to the possibilities of floating your own contemporary image or arrangement of blocks within this dramatic border. The high-contrast geometric blocks add depth to any quilt design and invite the viewer in for a closer look. Barbara Olson shares her technique to make this powerful and hypnotic background easy to create. The fabric choices are simple and the tools needed are few, but the results are out of this world!

Getting Ready

This checkerboard border directs your eye to the center design and gives the illusion of depth. The center of the quilt top appears to be floating or receding. Start by deciding on a scale for your checkerboard that won't overwhelm the central image. Some extremely bold, dynamic tops work well when supported by a larger checkerboard; other more intricate designs stand out better on a smaller one. Audition the proportions by cutting strips of light and dark fabrics and laying them next to the top.

Be sure that you prewash, thoroughly rinse, dry, and press your fabrics. (Dark-color fabrics especially should be rinsed until all excess dye is out and the rinse water runs clear.)

Drafting your checkerboard is much easier if you use large sheets of graph paper that you don't have to tape together. A 27 × 32-inch flip chart with 1-inch squares is perfect for most borders; check an office supply store for one of these.

What You'll Need

Quilt top

Two high-contrast fabrics for checkerboard

1-inch graph paper

Pencil

Fine-point permanent marker

Sulky Totally Stable or freezer paper

Iron and ironing board

Rotary cutting equipment

Pins

Sewing machine

Dark thread

Thread snips or embroidery scissors

Drafting the Checkerboard

1

Measure your quilt top center both vertically and horizontally. If it has intentionally curved or uneven edges, use the shortest measurement in each direction. Next, decide how wide you want your border to be. A good rule of thumb is to size your borders so their finished width is about one-half of the shortest side of your finished quilt center. The samples in this chapter start with a 12-inch finished quilt top center (not including seam allowances), and show how to make a 6-inch-wide checkerboard border to surround it. The finished quilt will measure 24 inches square.

2

Use 1-inch graph paper to draw a pattern that is one-quarter of your finished quilt, including borders. (Imagine you are dividing your quilt in half both horizontally and vertically.) You will create templates from this pattern, and you'll use each template piece four times. In the sample, the 6-inch finished border around a 12-inch center will have three rows of checkerboard, each 2 inches wide. **To begin drafting the pattern, first draw a 12-inch square on the graph paper. Then draw a 6-inch square for the quilt center and two L-shaped lines 2 inches apart for the checkerboard border.**

3

To draft the angled lines for the dimensional perspective, draw a tick mark every 2 inches along the bottom and right-hand edges of your square. Draw lines from each tick mark to the upper left-hand corner. Erase the lines inside the top left square (the quilt center). **Darken the remaining lines with a fine-point permanent marker.**

Label the outer segments of each "column," beginning at the edges of your drawing. **Label the horizontal row 1A through 6A, and the vertical row 1B through 6B.**

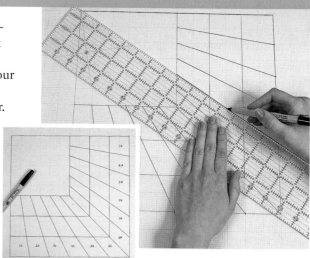

Making the Templates

Tape a piece of Sulky Totally Stable (or freezer paper) shiny side up over your graph paper drawing. **Trace all the lines and labels onto the foundation material with a fine-point permanent marker.**

Cut apart the traced pattern along the column lines, dividing it into 12 three-unit templates. To avoid confusion and lost templates, clip your templates together in two sets: 1A through 6A, and 1B through 6B.

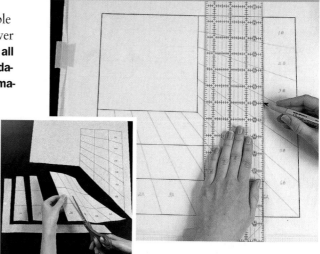

Constructing the Checkerboard

Cut strips of light and dark high-contrast fabrics as wide as the finished width of one checkerboard row, plus ½ inch for seam allowances. (In our example, each row is 2 inches wide, so the strips are cut 2½ inches wide.)

Make two types of strip sets: one with a dark strip between two light strips, and one with a light strip between two dark strips. For each type, you need a total length equal to the total border length around all four finished sides (in this example, 4 × 24 = 96 inches). Sew with a ¼-inch seam allowance, then press toward the dark fabric.

Tip

Sew with thread that matches the darker of your two fabrics; any show-through will be less distracting than light thread on a dark fabric.

Place both strip sets right side down on your ironing board. Pick up templates 1A through 6A. Beginning with template 1A on the dark-light-dark strip set, place the templates shiny side down on the strip sets, alternating strip sets. Repeat with templates 1B through 6B, beginning with 1B on the light-dark-light strip set and alternating strip sets. **Align the drawn horizontal lines on the templates with the seam lines in the strip sets;** leave at least ½ inch between templates for seam allowances. Press the templates onto the strip set using a dry iron on the cotton setting.

Tip

Templates 1A, 3A, 5A, 2B, 4B, and 6B will be on the dark-light-dark set. Templates 2A, 4A, 6A, 1B, 3B, and 5B will be on the light-dark-light strip set.

Using a rotary cutter and acrylic ruler, **cut out each template, adding ¼ inch for seam allowances along the sides** (you should already have ¼-inch seam allowances along the top and bottom). Pile the A and B pieces in numerical order in separate piles to prepare for pinning and sewing the two border segments that comprise each quarter of the border.

DEEP SPACE CHECKERBOARDS

4

Place pieces 1A and 2A right sides together, 1A on the bottom, 2A on the top, and the raw edges even. **Insert a pin straight through piece 2A, at the intersection of the sewn seam and the template's edge. Continue through piece 1A, at the intersection of the sewn seam and the template's edge.**

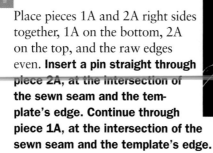

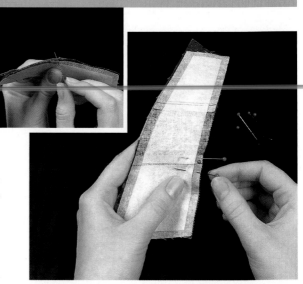

Keeping the first pin in place, **pin the pieces together ¼ inch on either side of the intersection.** Remove the first pin. Repeat and pin at each of the sewn seams to produce neat, crisp intersections in the checkerboard. Also pin at both ends of each segment.

5

Sew the pieces together, stitching exactly along the edges of the templates. Press toward the higher-numbered piece. **Continue adding pieces in order** until one segment is complete, then repeat, using the B pieces. Remove the templates, heating them slightly with the iron to loosen them.

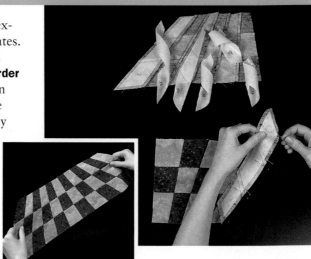

Repeat Steps 4 and 5, reusing the templates to construct the remaining three quarters of your checkerboard border. **Sew together two sections to form one complete side of your checkerboard border.**

6

If your quilt top has straight edges, arrange all the pieces on a flat surface. Sew a checkerboard border to each side of the quilt top, then miter the corners carefully. Match the seams along the angled border edges, pinning and sewing so the seams match for a neat miter.

For a quilt top with uneven or curved edges, sew the four borders together, then appliqué the top to the border.

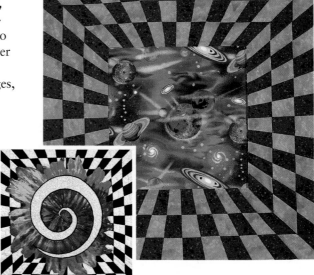

The Quilter's
Problem Solver

Keeping Imperfections in Check

Problem	Solution
My quilt has mismatched seams, puckers, and bunched-up sections. What am I doing wrong?	Templates must stay solidly pressed to the section. If you notice any part of the template coming loose in any phase of the process, immediately and accurately reposition it and re-press.
Help! My dark fabric shows through where strip set segments are joined and seams are pressed toward the light fabric.	You can avoid shadow-through a few different ways: ❑ Trim the dark fabric in the seam allowance where it shows through. Clip the dark fabric to about ⅛ inch, and it should hide behind the light fabric in the seam allowance. ❑ Choose only high-quality, tightly woven light fabric. ❑ Try using a tone-on-tone print for your light fabric. This often helps disguise show-through from darker fabrics.

Skill Builder

Practice makes precise.

Any variation in drafting, pinning, or sewing can throw off your checkerboard symmetry. For guaranteed results each time, follow these tips.

❑ Draft with a fine lead pencil and clear acrylic ruler, drawing a thin, even, straight line.

❑ Cut carefully when adding a precise ¼-inch seam around your templates. Use a sharp rotary cutter, and hold the ruler firmly in place.

❑ Sew a consistent ¼-inch seam allowance throughout.

❑ Hold your layers firmly in place when pinning.

❑ Press with a light touch; dragging the iron across seams can distort them.

Try This!

Heighten the drama of your checkerboard border.

Substitute a color gradation fabric for the dark fabric. Place the lightest tones on the outside row, a medium tone in the middle, and the darkest on the inside row. Position your templates carefully on your strip sets for a spectacular effect of gradually darker tones receding into deep space.

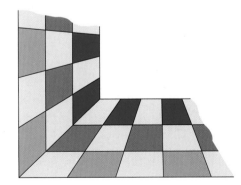

Throw Tradition
a Curve

I f you love traditional patterns but want to give them a bit of a "twist," why not give
Virginia Walton's Creative Curves Quilting System a try? Using her specially designed
rulers, you can turn any half-square or half-rectangle design into a curving, twirling
design, all without hassle or the laborious pinning of cantankerous curves! Just a few stitches
at a time will bring you precocious pinwheels, swooping half-square triangles, and more.

Getting Ready

This ingenious system uses a single, special ruler to cut all the shapes you need in order to substitute curved patches for triangles. Here, you will learn how to make curved triangle squares and a modified Flying Geese Pinwheel. Practice on these, and then move on to more complex combinations.

When cutting, you will first cut squares or rectangles, then cut those into curved pieces. The markings on the ruler help you align and cut your pieces: Solid black lines are seam lines; always align the outside edge of the curve with the outside raw edge of your cut square or rectangle. The rulers and quilt patterns are available through Creative Curves; see "Resources" on page 126 for ordering information. The ruler shown in this chapter produces 3-inch units; a ruler that produces 2-inch units is also available. To cut your curves accurately, use a rotary cutter with a small blade (28 mm) that will easily cut the inside curves.

What You'll Need

Creative Curves Ruler

Small (28 mm) rotary cutter

Cutting mat

Prewashed, pressed fabrics

Sewing machine

Thread to match fabrics

Iron and pressing surface

Stiletto, tailor's awl, or long, straight pin (optional)

Modified Triangle Square

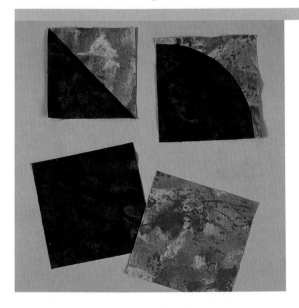

1

A triangle square is constructed from two half-square triangles sewn together along their long edges. **This innovative technique replaces the straight seam and substitutes a curved one.** To begin, choose two high-contrast fabrics: a dark background fabric and a lighter focus fabric. Cut a 3½-inch square from each fabric.

2

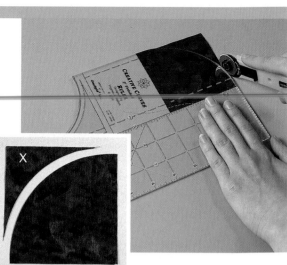

To cut the background square, use the outside (convex) curve on the ruler. Place the background right side up on a cutting mat. **Align the two outer solid black lines with two edges of the square,** so that the fabric shows through the shape that you will be cutting. Use a small rotary cutter to cut along the curve. **Discard the small curved corner that you cut off (labeled with an X),** and keep the pie wedge–shaped piece of fabric.

3

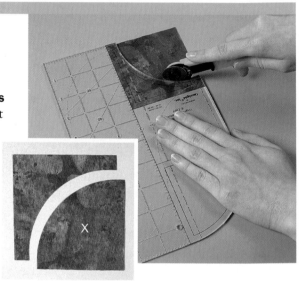

To cut the contrasting focus fabric, use the inside (concave) curve on the ruler. Place the square right side up on the cutting mat. **Align the two outer solid black lines with two edges of the square,** again making sure that the fabric shows through the shape that you will be cutting. To avoid having to twist your wrist while cutting, cut along the curve for about 1 inch on each end of the curve, then cut away the center of the curve. **Discard the pie wedge–shaped piece (labeled with an X),** or add it to your scrap bin.

4

Place the contrasting piece right side up on your sewing machine, so it forms an L. Align the background right side down on top, with the square corner at top left. Align the top right corner of the background with the top right corner of the L. **Place a finger about ½ inch from where you will begin sewing.**

Using ¼-inch seam allowances, sew three to five stitches. Stop sewing with the needle down, and **gently pull the pieces toward each other, holding them about ½ inch in front of the presser foot.** When the edges align, sew a few stitches, stop, realign the edges, and continue to sew the entire seam. Press toward the darker fabric.

Curved Flying Geese Pinwheel

This curved version of a Flying Geese Pinwheel is made up of four identical units: a square made up of three curved patches. First, choose a background fabric and a contrasting fabric that will form the pinwheel.

Cut rectangles as follows to make one block: **From the background, cut four that are 3½ × 6½ inches and two that are 3½ × 10¼ inches; from the contrasting fabric, cut two 3½ × 10¼-inch rectangles.** (Each 10¼-inch-long rectangle will yield two cut pieces.)

Tip

A Flying Geese Pinwheel is usually constructed from units made of one Flying Geese unit plus a same-size rectangle.

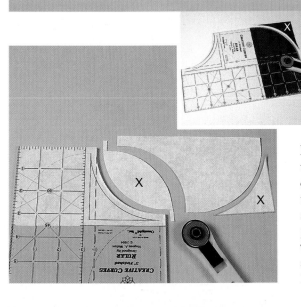

Place the short background vertically, right side up on the mat. Place the convex curve of the ruler at top right. **Cut along the curve; discard the cut-off corner.**

Position the long background horizontally, right side up. Holding the ruler vertically, align its top left corner with the strip's top left corner. Cut the concave curve. Rotate the mat 180 degrees, realign, and cut an identical shape. Discard the center piece. **Repeat with the contrasting rectangle,** *then* **cut outer curves at opposite ends** (shown outlined in orange). Discard pieces labeled with an X.

Tip

The pieces you cut from the long background strip will look like the uncut green one at the left side of the larger photo.

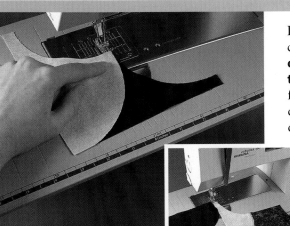

Place the background with the concave curve right side up. **Align the contrasting patch on top, right sides together, as shown.** Sew three to five stitches. Stop with the needle down, align the edges for a short distance, and sew the seam in this manner. Press toward the pinwheel fabric.

Position the remaining background right side up with the square corner to the left. **Align the contrasting fabric right side down, with the narrow part of the curve at the top right of the background.** Sew, then press.

Tip

Make four units and sew them together to make the Pinwheel block.

THROW TRADITION A CURVE

A Quick Route
to Drunkard's Path

One of the most popular pieced blocks, the Drunkard's Path breaks away from the straight and narrow with its winding curves. But piecing curves can be slow-going, painstaking work, as you must coerce concave and convex curves to fit together. Here's a fast and easy way to bypass all that work: "piece" your blocks with machine appliqué, then cut them into quarters. Go full-speed ahead toward any of the dozens of setting variations that the Drunkard's Path block lends itself to.

Getting Ready

With this technique, instead of sewing a concave curve to a convex one to make a Drunkard's Path unit, you'll machine appliqué one piece of fabric to another—no twisting or coercing the fabric is needed to make the pieces fit!

This unusual method of creating circles inside of squares frees you from formulas and standard templates so you can make the background block and the inner circle any size you want. (Some guidelines for deciding on the background and circle dimensions, plus measurements for a specific example, are included in the directions.)

You will need to "draft" your own template, but all that entails is drawing a circle onto template material. You don't have to worry about drafting curves that will fit together or adding seam allowances. You simply need to decide what size blocks you want to make, open your compass to the appropriate size, and draw a circle on the template plastic.

Four Units at Once

1

With this method, you sew a complete circle to a background square first using reverse appliqué by machine. Then you cut the square into four identical Drunkard's Path units.

To determine the finished size for your large background square, double the desired finished size of each individual Drunkard's Path unit, and add 1 inch for seam allowances. For instance, if you want 4-inch finished units, 4 × 2 = 8 inches, plus 1 inch for seam allowances, so you'll need to **cut 9-inch background squares.**

Tip

You may wish to cut the background squares extra large at this stage, then trim them down and square them up after adding the circle.

73

2

Use a compass to draw a circle onto template plastic. Your circle must be at least 1 inch smaller than your large background square. For a 9-inch square, a good size for a circle template is 6½ to 7½ inches in diameter; set your compass to span half the desired measurement. Draw the circle and cut out the template.

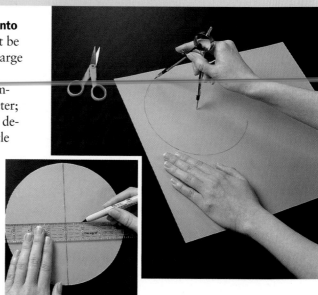

Mark guidelines on the circle to make it easier to center it on your background square. Mark the center of the template by drawing a line through the center point. Draw a second line perpendicular to the first, also through the center.

Tip

A see-through acrylic ruler makes it easy to draw a line perpendicular to the first one.

3

Fold the background square in half in both directions to make quarters. Lightly press along the fold lines just enough to crease these positioning lines. Unfold the fabric right side up and place the circle template over it, **aligning the marked guidelines on the circle with the creases on the fabric** to ensure that the circle is centered. Press down firmly on the template to hold it in place, and **draw around the circle with a fabric marking pencil.**

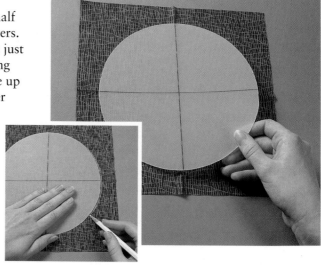

Tip

Lay the fabric square on your rotary cutting mat for tracing. The mat will grip the fabric enough to prevent it from shifting as you trace.

4

With fabric scissors, cut away the *inside* of the drawn circle from your background square, cutting approximately ¼ inch to the inside of the marked line. The marked line will serve as your turn-under line for the machine appliqué. **With embroidery scissors, clip into the curve all the way around the circle, at approximately ¼-inch intervals.** Do not cut right up to the marked line, only to within two or three threads of it.

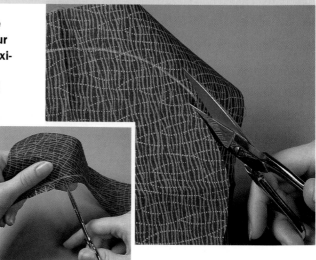

Tip

For smaller circles, clip at closer intervals; for larger circles, clip at intervals that are slightly farther apart.

For the circle inset fabric, **cut a square of your chosen fabric that is at least 1 inch larger than the diameter of the circle template.** For instance, if your circle template is 7 inches in diameter, cut an 8-inch square.

Lay the background square with the hole in it right side down on your table. **Lay the contrasting square right side down on top, so that it completely covers the hole.** Pin the square in place along the outer edges so the pins won't get in the way when you stitch.

Tip

You can also use odd-shaped scraps for your circle inset fabric; just be sure that the fabric completely covers the drawn turn-under line.

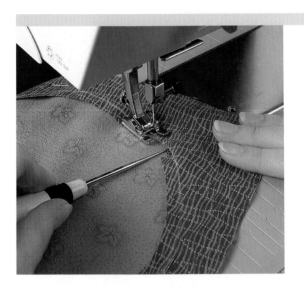

Set your sewing machine to a narrow zigzag stitch, and adjust the stitch length to about 14 stitches per inch (1.5 on European machines). Thread monofilament into the needle (clear for light fabrics; smoke for dark fabrics), and cotton thread in the bobbin. Turn the background square right side up. Start sewing near a corner, where there's more fabric to hold and guide through the machine. **Turn under about ½ inch of the background fabric along the marked line.** Use a tailor's awl or large needle to help turn under the seam allowance.

Tip

Remember to use an open-toe or appliqué foot for zigzag stitching (using a ¼-inch patchwork foot would break your needle!).

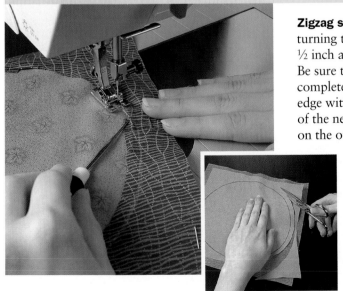

Zigzag stitch around the entire circle, turning the seam allowance under ½ inch ahead of the needle as you go. Be sure to turn the marked line under completely. Straddle the folded-under edge with your stitches: On one swing of the needle, enter the circle fabric; on the other swing, enter the seam allowance. When you get completely around the circle, backstitch and clip the threads.

Turn the block wrong side up. **Cut away the excess fabric from the smaller square,** leaving a ¼-inch seam allowance.

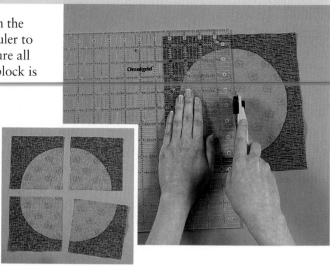

Press the completed block from the right side. Use a large square ruler to square up the block, making sure all the edges are straight and the block is truly square.

To cut the stitched block into four Drunkard's Path units, lay it on your rotary cutting mat. **Measure carefully, and cut the block in half both lengthwise and crosswise. This will yield four equal block quarters, or Drunkard's Path units.**

Design Variations

By combining your Drunkard's Path units into different arrangements, you can create both traditional and innovative designs. With this technique, you lose some of the circle's arc in seam allowances when you assemble your quilt top; this loss is more noticeable with circles less than 2 inches in radius that you put together to form whole circles. In that case, use ½-inch sashing strips to visually give

the feeling of a perfectly round circle. In any case, try sashing, or set the units together without it; mix and match colors, or stick to a planned scheme. Piece the units back together in the traditional Drunkard's Path arrangement, or combine mismatched circles for a fun and whimsical look. Bear in mind: There's no rule that says all your circles have to be the same size. Experiment and have fun!

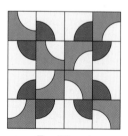

Traditional
Drunkard's Path

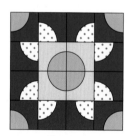

Harvest
Moon

Fool's
Puzzle

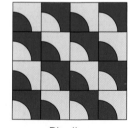

Rippling
Water

Bow Ties

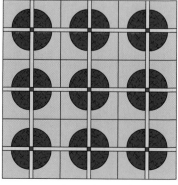

Polka Dots

The Quilter's
Problem Solver

Smooth Sewing

Problem	Solution
Sewing with monofilament causes puckers or thread "nests" to build up on your fabric.	Loosen the upper thread tension *only* when stitching with monofilament. If you have a numbered tension system, set it at a lower number. If your tension isn't numbered, turn the knob to the left (counterclockwise) to loosen the tension. Remember to reset it when you go back to using cotton thread. Try sewing with a temporary stabilizer such as Easy Tear underneath your fabric. This will help eliminate puckers and ease tension problems with your sewing machine.
My circle doesn't look perfectly round after sewing.	Don't worry! Once you cut the block into quarters and arrange the units in different patterns, small bumps or dents in the circle won't be noticeable. To help make your Drunkard's Path units smoother, use the tip of a round wooden toothpick to gently nudge the edges under before you sew. The slightly rough wood will grasp the fabric and help you turn it under. Crease the turned-under edge with your fingernail, and stitch.

Skill Builder

Once you become proficient at sewing smooth curves, embellish and emphasize the curve in one of the following ways:

❏ Madeira's wooly Burmilana thread, blanket-stitched by machine, will give you a folk art look.

❏ Satin-stitched rayon thread in a complementary color will add a subtle shimmer.

❏ Couch decorative cording or braid along the curve: Zigzag over the cord or braid with mono-filament as you stitch. Start and end at the mid-point of one side of the square to hide the ends in the seam allowances.

Try This!

Remember that recycling applies in the sewing room, too.

Save the fabric circles you cut away from your background square to use in other patchwork. Or, use them to make smaller Drunkard's Path blocks. They're perfect for fitting behind smaller circular openings on fabric squares. That way, while you're piecing larger blocks for a quilt, you'll have ready-made pieces to start on a small wallhanging or miniature companion piece.

Strip Piecing
Random Curves

Making wonderfully original, abstract quilts just came within reach, even for those of us with absolutely no artistic confidence. Sonya Lee Barrington's easy and achievable curved piecing is very much like the traditional strip-piecing technique, with one very obvious difference: Instead of piecing straight strips, you piece gently curved ones. Out of these meandering bands you can cut backgrounds, blocks, patches, sashings, or borders for a stunner of a quilt.

Getting Ready

Choose fat quarters (18 × 22-inch pieces of fabric) that reflect the feeling you want to create with your quilt. If you want a piece with high contrast, choose lights and darks, and omit medium tones. For a subtle piece, use colors similar in value to each other. Using only 100 percent cotton fabrics will give you the best results. Prewash and press your fabrics. Arrange them in the sequence that you wish to piece them. Sonya Lee Barrington uses her own hand-dyed cottons; see "Resources" on page 126.

The most important tool in this technique is a sharp rotary cutter. Follow good safety habits: Close the blade cover when you are not cutting, and always cut away from your body. To cut your curves, pretend you are drawing with the rotary cutter, and move along the fabric in a gentle curving line. Work on the largest-size cutting mat you have; 18 × 24 inches is optimal.

Five to eight fat quarters

Dark and light fabric-marking pencils

Straight pins

Fabric scissors

45 mm rotary cutter

Large rotary cutting mat (at least 18 × 24 inches)

Acrylic ruler

Sewing machine

Neutral thread

Iron and ironing board

Freehand Curves

 1

Position your cutting mat vertically, with the short edges at the top and bottom. Place your first fat quarter right side up, starting at the left edge of your cutting mat. Position the selvage along either the top or the bottom edge of the mat so that you can cut your curved strips along the crosswise grain. Crosswise grain has a bit more stretch than lengthwise grain, and this will work to your advantage when you join your curved edges. **Layer the second fabric on top of the first, also right side up, leaving about 3 inches of the first piece showing along the left edge.**

Tip

Reserve an older cutting mat for cutting curves. Curved cuts don't "heal" and your mat will become less useful for straight rotary cutting.

STRIP PIECING RANDOM CURVES

79

Tip

When deciding how wide to cut your curved strips, be aware that you'll be losing only ⅛ inch for each seam allowance.

Using a medium-size (45 mm) rotary cutter, start cutting slowly, away from your body. **Make a long, freehand cut, gently curving in and out, close to the left edge of the top fabric.** Discard the small sliver of the top fabric that you cut off. Remove the bottom fabric and set it aside. The left edge of this first fabric should remain uncut to provide a straight side for the finished strip set.

Tip

Always remove the bottom fabric and add a new top fabric after each cut.

Position the third fabric on top of the second, right side up. Leave 1 to 3 inches of the bottom fabric showing at the left edge. **Make a second gently curving cut, staying fairly close to the edge of the top fabric for minimal waste.** Set the second (bottom) curved strip aside with the first fabric strip, keeping them positioned in the order you cut them.

Continue layering and cutting two fabrics at a time until you have enough curved strips to make a strip set, or band, as wide as you desire. Cut the right edge of your last strip straight.

Tip

With this technique, it's best to avoid sharp curves. To sew sharp curves, see "Triumphant Arches" on page 96.

Experiment with different widths for the strips, as well as with slightly deeper and shallower curves. Variation in strip width gives interest to the completed band, while strips cut to roughly the same width produce a more uniform look once they are sewn together. Cutting your curves roughly parallel to each other lends a consistency to the band, while random curves will result in a quilt design that's a little less tame. A band can be made up of as few as two strips or as many strips as you wish.

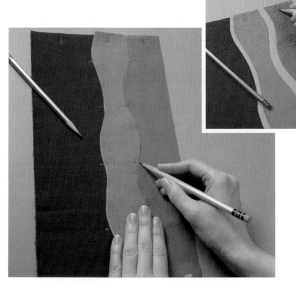

Once all your strips are cut, line them up next to each other with their wrong sides up. **Number the strips in sequence, marking the top edge of each strip.** Nest the matching curves, those that were cut together through two layers. Use a light or dark fabric marking pencil so your marks will show on your fabrics. **Draw short lines—registration marks—every 3 inches or so across the edges as an aid for matching pieces.** Make these marks perpendicular to the cut edges.

Tip

Label and mark your fabrics on a cutting mat. The surface will grip the fabrics in place as you write.

Pick up the first two strips and place them right sides together. Pin them together, lining up registration marks on the edges and placing a pin at each one. **Align the raw edges halfway between the registration marks, and pin there.** Continue pinning between pins until you have four to six pins between each mark (more for tighter curves, fewer for gentler curves). Place the pins perpendicular to the sewing line and as close to the cut edge as possible. Take just a tiny "bite" with each pin; this will allow the curves to bend and flex as you sew.

Tip

Position the heads of the pins away from the fabric so you can easily remove pins as you sew.

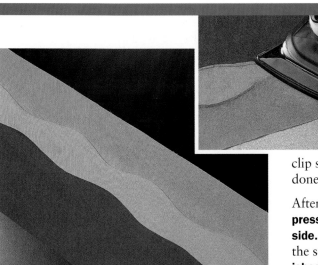

Set your sewing machine to sew about 14 stitches per inch. Sew the strips together ⅛ inch from the raw edges, removing the pins as you come to them. (This narrow seam allowance will keep you from having to clip seam allowances after you're done sewing.)

After all the strips have been added, **press the entire band from the wrong side.** Use a hot, dry iron, and press all the seams in one direction **so the finished band will lie flat.**

Tip

A shorter stitch length produces smoother curves and will hold the seam together when you cut across it later.

STRIP PIECING RANDOM CURVES

Using Your Curved Bands

Borders

Tip

If you want the inner edge of your border to be curved as well, topstitch the curve to your quilt top (see page 84).

Your curved bands are naturals for use as borders. Make bands longer than the sides of your quilt top, then **audition the curved strips against the quilt top on your design wall.** Try mitering the corners, folding the bands at 45-degree angles and sliding one band up or down slightly until the seam lines match nicely at the corner.

If you like the wavy look, why not cut curves along the outside edges of your border bands? Then bind the curved edges of your quilt with bias binding.

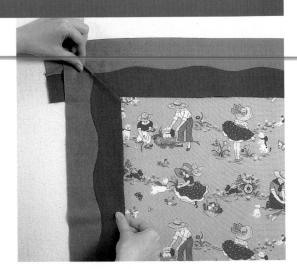

Blocks

Tip

To stabilize bias edges when bands are cut on the diagonal, staystitch close to the edges before sewing pieces together.

Cut unique blocks from the curved bands. Use a rotary cutter and ruler to cut strips along the grain or on the diagonal. Try to cut the pieces so there are no seams at the corners (the extra seam allowances will add up to bulky, bumpy intersections when you join blocks). Play with various arrangements. **Set them next to each other, turning them different ways to create a sense of motion and various patterns.** Or alternate your blocks with plain blocks. When you are satisfied with a design, assemble the blocks to make your quilt.

Patches

Tip

Play with your curve-pieced patches and plain fabrics on your design wall to discover combinations that you couldn't have planned or imagined.

Cut smaller patches from your curved bands. **Use clear templates or window templates to view your patches before you cut;** different areas and angles will produce very different effects. Combine them with plain fabrics, or with each other. Cut triangles, squares, and rectangles both on grain and on the bias for different looks. By cutting your patches from curved bands, **the simplest quilt patterns, such as triangle squares, can yield the most complex-looking results.**

The Quilter's
Problem Solver

Solving Cutting Predicaments

Problem	Solution
The fabric crawls or moves along the cutting mat as you cut curves.	Your rotary cutter is dragging the fabric along with it as it cuts. Use a very sharp blade and cut slowly. In addition, place your noncutting hand on the lower edge of the fabrics below where you are cutting, and hold the layers firmly in place.
There are nicks or uneven cuts along the edges of the fabric strips.	Recut the uneven part of the top fabric, then relayer the two fabrics, both right side up. Use the newly cut edge as a guide to cut and correct the unevenness on the second piece. Both strips will be a bit narrower than before, but you will still be able to use them.

Skill Builder

Practice makes perfect.

Most quilters are used to making straight cuts along a ruler with a rotary cutter. To help master the skill of cutting smooth curves without wasting your fabric stash, try it out on paper first. Use an old cutting mat and an old blade in your rotary cutter. (Curved cuts don't "heal" and will ruin your good mat. Likewise, cutting paper will dull the blade of your rotary cutter and make it unsuitable for cutting fabric.) Layer construction paper or colored photocopy paper as you would fabric, and practice your gentle curved cuts until you're confident enough to use this technique on fabric.

Try This!

Learn the right way to cut long strips.

If you're interested in longer borders or 42-inch-wide pieced "yardage," you'll need to cut strips from selvage to selvage across the whole width of the fabric. Fold the fabric right sides together, matching the selvages carefully and precisely, and place the fold nearest your body. Cut straight for at least ½ inch, then begin your curved cut; otherwise, you'll cut a sharp angle instead of a curve at the fold.

Topstitched
Curves

reeform curves, like these by Karen Eckmeier, are as easy to stitch as they are to draw. There's no fussing with templates or freezer paper, no need for careful clipping, and only limited planning and pinning required! Use the abstract results of this technique for layers of sea, sky, or land; or make them into waves, sand, rolling hills, or wind. Create your own one-of-a-kind fabric collage, add movement to a landscape, or build an unusual border with these topstitched curves.

Getting Ready

Decide on a theme that you would like to capture in curved lines. Choose fabrics to reflect the color, texture, and mood of your theme. For a watery theme, choose hand-dyed or batik fabrics in blues and greens; for a landscape of mountains, choose deep, dark, richly textured fabrics. Choose values that range from very light to very dark. The amount of fabric you need will depend on your project, but as a general guide, you'll use ½ yard each of six different fabrics to make a curved creation of about 18 × 22 inches. Cut your ½-yard pieces into four more manageable 9 × 22-inch pieces to begin. Or, work with pieces up to 12 inches wide to create smaller blocks. The fabrics should all be the same width.

Topstitched piecing creates an overlaid, dimensional effect without the bulk of many layers. If you topstitch your curves all in the same direction, you get the effect of moving up or down a hill. You can create a deliberate "valley," or low spot, by working from both sides toward the middle. Or, you can create a "ridge," or high spot, by working from the middle out to both sides. Read on to see how you can achieve these effects.

What You'll Need

½ yard each of six fabrics, ranging from light to dark

Rotary cutter

Old cutting mat

Chalk pencil or tailor's chalk

Iron and ironing board

Glass-headed pins

Sewing machine

Thread to match fabrics

Fabric scissors

Topstitch Piecing in One Direction

1

Arrange your fabrics in order from dark to light on a work surface. To do this, it's very helpful to look through a value finder. A value finder is a piece of red transparent acrylic that lets you ignore the color of the fabrics and instead concentrate on their relative value to each other.

Tip

If you are working with red fabrics, use a green value finder.

Tip

Keep an old rotary mat (or the reverse side of a good mat) for cutting curves. Curved cuts don't "heal," even on a self-healing mat.

 2

Place either the lightest or the darkest fabric right side up on your rotary mat. **With the rotary cutter, cut a gentle curve.** If you're not sure what shape curve you want or you're wary of cutting freehand, **you might want to experiment first by marking lines on your fabric with a chalk pencil or tailor's chalk.** To erase lines you don't want, dampen them lightly with water. Cut along the lines you like.

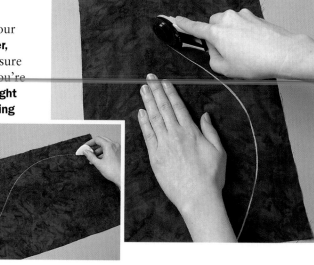

Tip

Think of the iron as a helicopter hovering over the fabric, touching down only very lightly as your fingers move on ahead.

3

Place your fabric right side down on the ironing board. With your thumb on top and index finger underneath, lightly roll and pinch a ¼-inch seam allowance to the wrong side along the curved, cut edge. **Slide your thumb and finger slowly along the edge, pinching the seam allowance under and then following with the iron in your other hand,** *gently* **pressing the seam allowance down.** The fabric doesn't need to be pressed completely flat, just creased along the fold.

4

Place your second fabric right side up on your cutting mat. Position the first piece right side up on top, with the turned-under seam allowance overlapping the second fabric. **Make sure that the curved pressed edge overlaps the second fabric along the entire length of the curve.** Align the side edges of the fabric strips.

Cut a curve along the length of the second piece of fabric, echoing the general shape of the first fabric's curve. Keep the cut at least ½ inch and not more than 1¼ inches from the folded edge of the first curve to keep the curved color bands in proportion to each other. For added interest, cut this new curve so that it varies slightly in width. If you prefer not to cut freehand, mark the curve in chalk first.

Pin the two layers of fabric together, placing pins about 2 inches apart. Pin from the folded edge in, keeping the heads of the pins outside the sewing line. This way, you can remove them easily as you sew.

Tip

Pins with large glass heads are especially easy to grab and remove as you sew.

Set your stitch length a bit longer than you would for regular piecing, 10 or 11 stitches per inch. Thread your machine with a color that closely matches the top fabric (we used a contrasting-color thread so you can see it better). Use a presser foot that allows you to easily see where you're sewing. Your line of stitching serves two purposes: It holds the layers together, and it also decorates the edge of the curve. **Sew the top fabric to the bottom one, stitching ⅛ inch inside the curved, folded edge.** Remove the pins as you come to them.

Tip

Position the needle ⅛" left of the center guide line, and keep the center aligned with the fold.

TOPSTITCHED CURVES

8

After the seam is sewn, turn your fabrics over. **Using sharp sewing scissors, trim the seam allowance to approximately ¼ inch** (cutting away the excess second fabric from behind the first). Press the seam from the front so **your curve will lie flat.**

Continue folding under the seam allowance, layering the next fabric, cutting the new curve, topstitching, trimming, and pressing until you have added all of your fabrics. Change threads to match fabrics; contrasting thread draws attention to the stitching, rather than the curve.

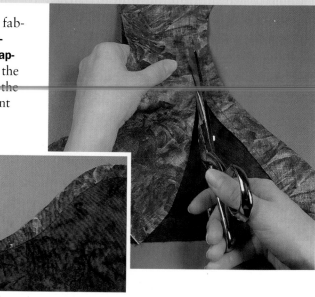

Creating a Valley

1

A valley is a "low spot." The valley fabric recedes from the adjoining fabrics as they overlap it on both sides. Arrange your fabrics in order, and decide which one will be your valley.

Cut, press, and topstitch your fabrics (see Steps 2 through 8 on pages 86 through 88) until you come to the one before the valley fabric. Cut a curve in its edge. Set the valley fabric aside and **use the cut curve as a guide to draw an identical curve on the fabric that will come *after* your valley,** to ensure the curve is echoed on either side of the valley. Cut along the marked line.

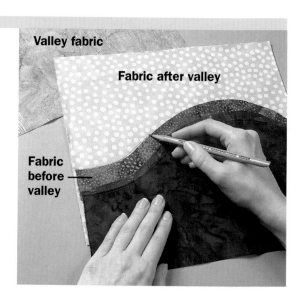

Valley fabric

Fabric after valley

Fabric before — valley

2

Pinch and press a ¼-inch seam allowance along the curve of the fabric that comes before the valley fabric. **Pin the curve to the valley fabric** and topstitch the seam ⅛ inch from the folded edge. Remove the piece from the sewing machine, and trim the excess valley fabric from underneath, leaving only ¼-inch seam allowances. Press the sewn seam.

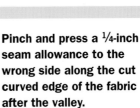

Pinch and press a ¼-inch seam allowance to the wrong side along the cut curved edge of the fabric after the valley.

Place your sewn piece on a work surface with the valley fabric facing away from you. Place the fabric after the valley on top. Align edges, and position the identical curves parallel and about ½ inch apart. **Experiment with the placement of the curves by shifting the fabric toward and away from its twin curve.** Once you find an arrangement you like, pin the edge in place on the valley fabric.

Tip

If the folded edges of your curves touch or even overlap at some point, it adds more interest and depth to your valley design.

Turn your work so you can sew from the opposite direction and so that the bulk of your piece is to the right, underneath the machine. **Sew the new curve to the valley fabric, topstitching ⅛ inch from the folded edge, as before.** Trim the seam allowance to ¼ inch, and press. Continue in this way **until you have added all your fabrics.**

Creating a Ridge

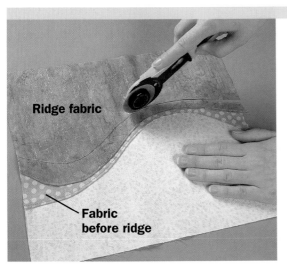

Ridge fabric

Fabric before ridge

A ridge is a "high spot." The ridge fabric stands out from its adjoining fabrics because it overlaps both of them. Lay your fabrics out in the order you wish to sew them, and decide which will be the ridge fabric.

Follow Steps 2 through 8 on pages 86 through 88 for cutting, pressing, and topstitching all pieces on one side, up to and including the ridge fabric. Then turn the piece so that the folded edges are on your left (if you're right-handed), **and mark with chalk or rotary cut the curve on the ridge fabric.**

TOPSTITCHED CURVES

2

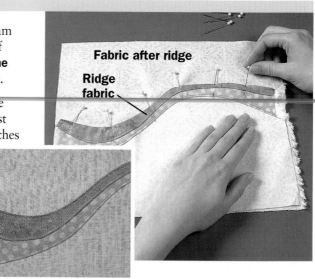

Fabric after ridge

Ridge fabric

Pinch and press under a ¼-inch seam allowance at the cut curved edge of the ridge fabric. **Pin this edge to the next fabric,** and topstitch as before.

Don't be concerned if the outer side edges of the ridge ruffle slightly. Just remove a few of the outermost stitches at the end of each line of stitching, re-press that section, then repin and resew, back-stitching a bit at either end to secure the stitching.

Press, trim, and continue adding fabrics **until your ridge piece is complete.**

Color for Topographical Effects

Combining ridges and valleys into one piece gives texture, motion, and excitement to your topstitched piece. **And by selecting and placing your colors carefully, you can create the illusion of a higher ridge and a lower valley.** In this piece, the dark tones in and around the valley make it appear to recede even further below its surrounding fabrics, while the lighter fabrics at the ridge make it seem to soar above the neighboring colors.

Piecing with Topstitched Curves

Try this easy, fun quilt project: Start with a large piece of yardage you create with topstitched curves. Vary the values and the use of valleys and ridges. When you're done, cut the yardage into smaller, similarly sized blocks. If you're feeling adventurous, do this freehand, without rotary rulers. Play around with these blocks on a design wall until you are satisfied with an arrangement. Sew the blocks into rows, then sew the rows together. Use topstitched curves to create the perfect border.

The Quilter's
Problem Solver

Hitches, Glitches & Jerks

Problem	Solution
Pressed curves are not smooth.	Cut gentler curves. Sharp curves or very high "bumps" in your curves are more difficult to sew smoothly. Concave curves are easier to iron than convex curves.
	Use a light touch when ironing the fabric edges under. If you press the fabric completely flat, you will create pleats and lumps.
	If you wait to manipulate the curve with your fingers when pinning, you'll get a more perfect curve. Using the tip of a pin or tweezers can also make this easier.

Skill Builder

Topstitch angles as well as curves.

Cut the angles you want to top-stitch into the edge of a piece of fabric. Angles greater than 90 degrees work best—there's less excess fabric to fold under. Clip about 3/16 inch into the inside angles, then turn under the seam allowance. Press under first one side of the angle and then the other, overlapping them with a fold. Use your angled pieces to add rocks and mountains to a landscape, or to surround an otherwise curvaceous design. Or, combine topstitched curves and angles in the same piece to create a wildly abstract work of art.

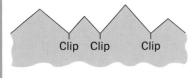
Clip   Clip   Clip

Try This!

Once you have the technique down, combine different colors, patterns, and techniques.

❑ When working with gradated value fabrics, start in the middle of your gradation with a medium value fabric and vary the placement of the lights and darks.

❑ To create a striped look, arrange your fabrics so that each one has a high level of contrast with its neighbors.

❑ For the most visual impact, choose high-contrast colors for valley and ridge fabrics.

❑ Combine valleys and ridges in the same piece for a quilt that really moves.

❑ Use a variegated thread when topstitching to add color, and to save time switching threads to match fabric.

❑ Play with contrasting color threads when topstitching, to give your curves extra visual impact.

TOPSTITCHED CURVES

91

A Feathered Sun
to *Let You Shine*

The Feathered Sun quilts that John Flynn makes are inspired by the Buffalo Robe Paintings of the Plains Indians. He creates concentric rings of triangles, like those used in the traditional Pickle Dish, New York Beauty, Rising Sun, and Wheel of Fortune quilting patterns. His technique uses strip sets as a shortcut when piecing these sharp points, and he uses no foundations. Follow the instructions in this chapter, and you, too, will be able to achieve effects similar to his shining example.

Getting Ready

John Flynn's technique combines strip piecing with templates to make rings of triangles. Follow the steps in this chapter to create the center portion of the quilt on the opposite page. Careful marking, accurate rotary cutting, and precise piecing are essential to this technique. Using the patterns on page 122, trace and cut accurate templates from high-quality template plastic. Or, consider making templates from a thicker, heavy plastic laminate material (available from John Flynn's Quilt Frame Company; see "Resources" on page 126). The heavier material is easier to use with a rotary cutter.

When making strip sets, cut strips carefully and sew them together with a scant ¼-inch seam allowance. For greatest accuracy, press after adding each strip.

Choose fabrics with good color contrast. Red, yellow, black, and white are used in the Little Red Cloud quilt on the opposite page to represent the four races of mankind and the four compass points in sacred Lakota ceremonies.

What You'll Need

- 1¼ yards background fabric (gray in the photo)
- ¼ yard each red and yellow fabrics for points
- Rotary cutting mat
- 24-inch acrylic ruler
- Small (28 mm) and medium (45 mm) rotary cutters
- Heavy template plastic
- Fine-point permanent marking pen
- Craft scissors
- Hole punch
- Pins
- Sewing machine
- Neutral thread
- Iron and pressing surface

Constructing a Feathered Sun

1

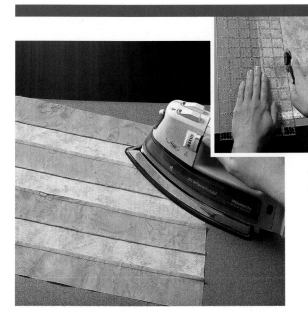

Begin by constructing the smaller feathered ring. To make the innermost ring (Ring A, made of background and yellow fabrics in the photo on the opposite page), make a strip set of your chosen fabrics.

Cut three strips from the point (yellow) fabric, each 2¼ × 20 inches. Cut four strips from the background fabric, each 1⅞ × 20 inches. Sew these into one strip set, beginning and ending with background strips, and alternating fabrics. **Press the seams toward the point (yellow) fabric.**

2

Very carefully trace the Ring A template on page 122 onto template material, and cut it out. Be sure to mark the diagonal seam line indicated on the pattern by the long dashed line, and **use a hole punch to make a hole where indicated.** You'll use the dashed diagonal line to line up the template with the seam on your strip set, and you'll use the hole to ensure that you have placed the template correctly on the fabrics.

3

Tip

Be very careful when cutting. You don't have the thick edge of an acrylic ruler next to your rotary cutter to protect the template *or* your fingers.

Lay your strip set on a cutting mat. **Place the Ring A template in the lower right corner so that the marked line on the template aligns with the sewn seam** and the point (yellow) fabric shows through the punched hole. Cut around the template with a small rotary cutter. **Rotate the template 180 degrees and place it just to the left of the first cut, so the dashed line falls on the next seam and the yellow fabric shows through the hole.** This makes most efficient use of your fabrics. Cut a total of 32 Ring A units in this manner.

4

Hold one unit right side up with the tip of the point (yellow) triangle pointing away from you. Place a second unit face down on top, with its point (yellow) tip also pointing away from you. **Align the raw edges at the side,** pin, and sew along the edge of the top yellow point, using a scant ¼-inch seam allowance. **Repeat, sewing units together in pairs.** Press all the seams toward the point (yellow) fabric as you go. Chain stitch pairs into 8 groups of 4, then 4 groups of 8, then 2 groups of 16. Sew the two resulting half-rings together to complete Ring A.

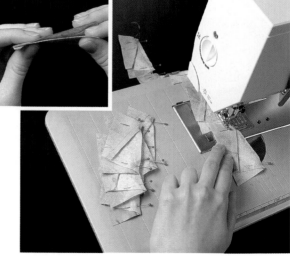

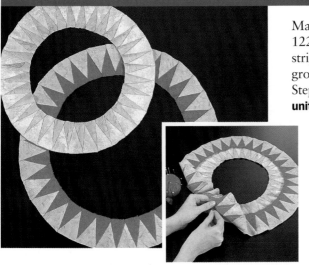

Make a Ring B template (see page 122). Cut three 2¼ × 20-inch red strips and four 2⅝ × 20-inch background strips. Make a strip set as in Step 1; cut 32 Ring B units. **Sew the units into a ring,** pressing toward the red point fabric.

Position Ring B on top of Ring A with right sides together. **Match points at the inner curve of Ring B to points at the outer curve of Ring A;** pin all around. Sew slowly and carefully ¼ inch from the edge; fold Ring B out. Press seam allowances lightly toward Ring B.

Tip

Handle the edges of your rings very carefully; they fray and stretch easily.

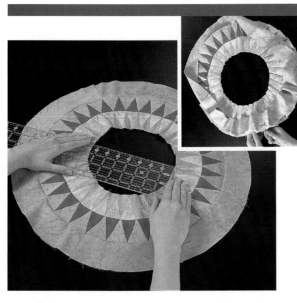

Make a Ring C template (see page 122). Cut eight C pieces from background fabric; sew them into a ring. **Place Ring C on top of Ring AB with right sides together; pin every fourth red point to a Ring C seam.** Add pins at each point in between. Sew, using a ¼-inch seam. Press seam allowances toward Ring C.

Measure across the center of the Ring A opening. It should measure 7½ inches. Use a compass to draw an 8½-inch center circle on fabric. If the opening is *not* 7½ inches, add 1 inch to its measurement, and draw a circle of that diameter. Cut out the circle.

Tip

When sewing pieced rings to plain ones, sew with the pieced ring on top so you can see the seam intersections and sew through them to make nice, sharp points.

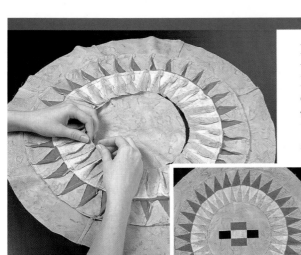

Fold your circle in half, into quarters, then again into eighths; finger-press light creases. **Pin the A ring to the center circle, matching up every fourth point to a crease.** Add pins in between until you're comfortable sewing the curve. Sew the circle to Ring A, using a ¼-inch seam allowance. Press the seam allowances towatd the center. **Appliqué a design in the center of the circle.**

You can consider your quilt top complete. Or, appliqué the circle to a background for a square quilt or a medallion center of a larger quilt or wallhanging.

Tip

You could also design a pieced circle to fill the center, like the center of Little Red Cloud on page 92.

A FEATHERED SUN TO LET YOU SHINE

Triumphant *Arches*

If the mere thought of sewing sharp curves sends shivers up your spine, check out Karen Eckmeier's freezer-paper template method for taming even the most vaulting arches. The secret is in the prep work. Careful marking and pinning will ensure the smoothest, most swooping lines. With this technique, you'll think nothing of including bold and dramatic curves in your next quilt.

Getting Ready

Decide on the curved design that you would like to piece, or trace the sample Arch Block on page 101. Inspiration for your design can be as close by as your most recent doodle. Sketch your design on paper and work with it, refining it until you are satisfied with what you've drawn. Use it at the size you've drawn, or enlarge it on a photocopier to the size you want.

When choosing fabrics for your arches, use colors or values with high contrast to best show off your curved-line designs. Plan fabric placement in advance so you know which fabrics will be adjacent to each other. Determine the best fabric marking tools to use for each fabric you've chosen. Test pens and pencils on a scrap of each fabric to make sure the lines will show up on the wrong side and won't bleed through to the right side.

What You'll Need

Drawn design, or copy of Arch Block pattern on page 101

Pencil

Freezer paper

Paper scissors

Iron and ironing board

Fabric scissors

Medium-point permanent fabric marker, such as a Pigma pen

Fabric marking pencils

Embroidery scissors

Silk pins (*without* glass heads)

Sewing machine

Neutral color thread

Sharp Curves Ahead

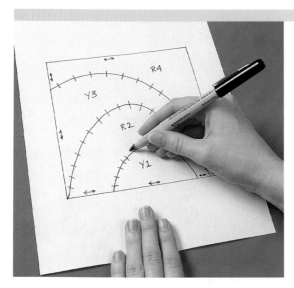

1

Label the individual pieces on your drawn or traced design. Label both the sewing order and the fabric designation. Begin numbering with the innermost piece of your arch, and number consecutively out to the outermost piece. Give each fabric a letter designation (such as R for red), and label each piece with its fabric code.

To help align the curves for accurate sewing later, mark them now with registration lines. **Draw short lines across and perpendicular to the curve about every ½ inch (even closer together where the curve is sharp).**

Tip

Mark pieces at the edges of the block with arrows to remind you to place the straight grain along those edges.

2

Tip

To reverse your pattern, use a light box or sunny window to retrace your design on the back of the paper.

If you want your finished block to look like your pattern, trace your design in reverse. Cut a piece of freezer paper that is 1 inch larger on all sides than your drawn design. Freezer paper makes ideal templates because it sticks to the fabric and does not shift easily when you trace around it. **Using a pencil, trace your drawn design onto the dull (nonwaxy) side of the freezer paper.** Transfer arrows, labels, and registration marks.

Carefully cut apart the freezer paper design along your drawn lines. Each piece will be a template that you will use to sew the Arch block.

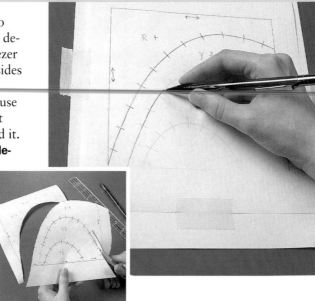

3

Tip

For a large design, tape pieces of freezer paper together, placing tape on the waxy side so it won't stick to your iron.

Place the waxy side of the freezer paper on the wrong side of the corresponding fabric, positioning outside edges marked with an arrow along the straight grain. **Iron each freezer paper template onto the fabric.** When ironing more than one template onto a fabric, leave at least ¾ inch between shapes, for seam allowances. After a few seconds of pressing with a dry, hot iron, the freezer paper will stick to your fabric. If a freezer paper template peels off before you want it to, simply iron it back on again.

4

Tip

Use scissors, not a rotary cutter, to cut sharp curves. Cutting curves will leave small nicks in your cutting mat.

Using fabric scissors, cut out each piece, leaving at least ¼ inch of fabric outside the freezer paper template. You can "eyeball" these seam allowances, but be generous: It's easier to trim excess fabric later than it is to try to fudge a too-narrow seam allowance. Leave at least ½ inch along edges that lie along the perimeter of the piece. Curved piecing can shrink and distort fabrics, and the extra fabric gives you a little margin for error when it's time to square up your sewn piece or block.

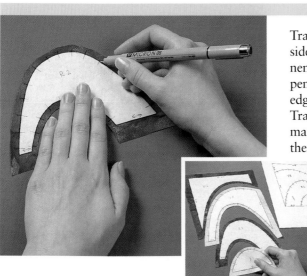

Trace the sewing lines onto the wrong side of each fabric piece. Use a permanent fabric marker (such as a Pigma pen), and trace around the outside edges of your freezer paper templates. Trace the corners first, being careful to mark them exactly so you can piece them precisely later. **Draw registration marks extending from the freezer paper marks into the seam allowance of each piece.**

Arrange your fabric pieces template side (wrong side) up in the order you will sew them. Refer to your original design if necessary.

Tip

Use a dark pen with a medium tip on medium-dark fabrics, a white pencil on dark fabrics, and a soft marking pencil for light fabrics.

Using sharp embroidery scissors, clip the concave (inner) curves between each registration mark. Clip up to within one or two threads of the sewing line, but not through it. This will help you ease in the piece as you sew the two curves together.

As you pin and sew, keep the piece of fabric with the concave (inner) curve on top so that you can get a smoother sewn curve.

Tip

An easy way to remember which curve is concave is to remember that it bends in, like a cave.

Pick up the first two pieces you will sew, and remove the freezer paper from both. Place them right sides together, with the concave curve on top.

Begin at a corner, and place a pin exactly through the marked corner point of your top piece, then through the corresponding marked corner point of your bottom piece. Pinch the pieces together tightly and pin the corner securely. **Place your pin so it points out, with the tip of the pin just inside your drawn sewing line.** This will hold your fabric in place, and you won't have to stop and remove pins as you sew. Remove the first pin from the corner.

Tip

Avoid sewing over pins. You'll have more secure stitches and smoother curves.

Tip

On tight curves, pin every ¼ inch, adding extra pins between registration lines.

8

Continue pinning along your curve. **First, place a pin exactly through the point where a registration mark intersects your drawn sewing line on both pieces. Pinch the fabric pieces together tightly to hold them in place, and then pin as shown, with the pin pointing out of the piece and the tip just inside the drawn sewing line.** Remove the first pin from the registration line, and continue pinning to the opposite corner, repeating Step 7 on page 99 at the corner.

Tip

To fix a small pleat or bobble, remove only the stitches that strayed from the sewing line or that encase a fold; then repin and resew that section.

9

When sewing curves, don't sew all the way to the edges of the fabric—sewing the seam allowance at the ends tends to distort your curve when you press your seam. Instead, begin sewing only one or two stitches outside the sewing line at the corner. **Sew slowly along the marked line and keep the fabric flat.**

End your line of stitching one or two stitches beyond the marked corner point, and remove the pins.

Tip

Don't drag your iron along the sewn seam; it will distort the curve.

10

Since you cut your pieces "eye-balling" the seam allowances, they may not match up exactly. **For a neater finish, use sharp sewing scissors to trim them so that they are even with each other.**

Place the pieces on your ironing board with the darker piece on top. Press the seam as it was sewn, to ease in any puckering that may have occurred when you were sewing. Then, gently open out the top (darker) piece and **press the seam flat.**

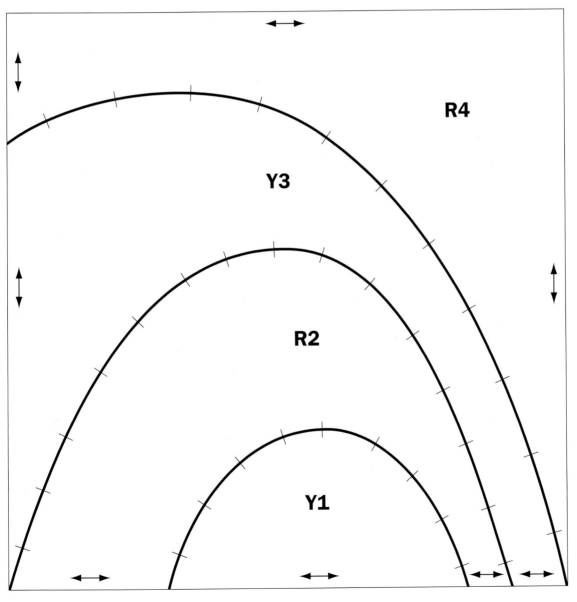

Continue adding your curved pieces in the same way. Press each seam as it is sewn, then open out and press toward the darker fabric. **When the block is complete, the curves on both the front and back should lie smooth and flat.**

R4

Y3

R2

Y1

Arch Block (Full-size)

Outstanding
Prairie Points

emember the humble little prairie point, used as a traditional edging? Well, quilt designer Jackie Robinson has much bigger plans for a troupe of them to take center stage. Follow her lead as she encases them in seams, then lets them flap as pinwheel points or stand out as star points in many variations. It all points to real dimension and excitement in your quilts.

Getting Ready

A prairie point is simply a square of fabric folded in half twice diagonally to form a quarter-square triangle. It has one fold on one side, two folds on another side, and four layers of raw edges along the base of the triangle.

This chapter showcases Jackie Robinson's favorite methods for incorporating prairie points into her piecing. When constructing units, you will sometimes machine-baste pieces together with ⅛-inch *security seams* to hold all the layers in place before you join them to other pieces. Because prairie points have four layers, they sometimes tend to shift while sewing a seam; the security seam prevents this. You'll sew security seams always looking at the *right* side of the fabrics, since you're basting pieces on top of each other.

Construction seams are the typical scant ¼-inch seams used to join the pieces of the block. When sewing a construction seam, you'll always be looking at the *wrong* side of the fabric.

What You'll Need

Fabric, prewashed, pressed, and cut into:

> **four 3½-inch squares for the background**

> **four 3½-inch squares for the prairie points**

Silk pins

Sewing machine

Thread to match fabrics

Prairie Point Pinwheel

1

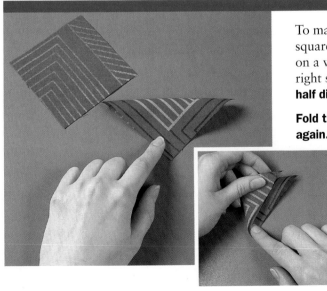

To make a basic prairie point, place a square of fabric (3½ inches square) on a work surface in front of you, right side down. **Fold the square in half diagonally.**

Fold the same piece in half diagonally again. Do not press the folds; the pieces should stay as softly three-dimensional as possible.

2

To make a prairie point pinwheel, you will need squares of a background fabric that are the same size as your original prairie point square (in this case, 3½ inches). Place a background square on your work surface, right side up. **Position a folded prairie point with its raw edges along the right edge of the square and with the tips of the double fold of the prairie point pointing toward the bottom edge of the background square.** Pin together if desired, and **sew together with a narrow ⅛-inch security seam.** Repeat to make a total of four of these prairie point units.

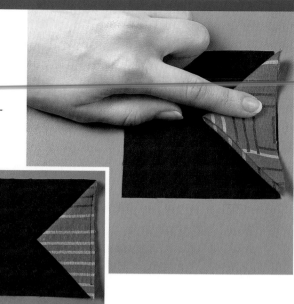

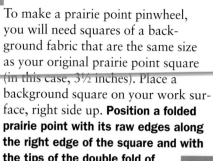

Tip

If the prairie point layers shift underneath the presser foot, begin stitching the security seam about ⅜ inch in from the edge of the prairie point.

3

Arrange four prairie point units into a Four Patch, with the tips of the open prairie point folds toward the center. Sew the units into pairs, using a scant ¼-inch seam. Use your fingers to coax the seam allowances toward the side with only one layer of fabric.

Sew the pairs together to form a pinwheel, taking care to match the center seams and sewing with ¼-inch seam allowances.

Tip

Choose fabrics with a high degree of contrast so that your pinwheel really "pops" off the background.

4

Clip the long seam allowances between the two pinwheel halves at the intersection, stopping just one or two threads shy of the stitching.

Using your fingers, **fan the seams** so the block will lie flat. Give the seam allowances a shot of steam if you find it necessary in order to coax them into position. Avoid pressing them flat, so the prairie points stay soft and dimensional.

Prairie Point Compass Star

1 Make four prairie point units, as shown in Steps 1 and 2 on pages 103 and 104. **Arrange the units on your work surface into a Pinwheel block, with the tips of the double-fold edge of the prairie points at the center of the new unit. Sew the units into pairs, using a scant ¼-inch seam allowance.** Follow Steps 3 and 4 on the opposite page.

Make as many blocks as you need.

2 Assemble your blocks into a quilt top; layer, baste, and quilt it. After quilting is complete, place the quilt top on your work surface. Select a Prairie Point Pinwheel block to work on first. Pick up one of the points and **insert one finger between the double folds to spread the prairie point open and create a hollow "cone." With your other hand, press down on the single fold so it aligns with the sewn seam.** Flatten the prairie point into a kite shape. Handle the edges gently so they don't crease.

Tip

When quilting, flip the prairie point flaps as needed so you can quilt the area on either side of them. Do not quilt through them!

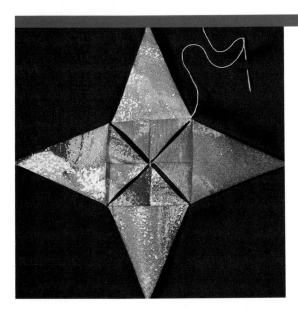

3 **Carefully hand tack the outer corners of the spread-out prairie points to the background and to each other,** so the new shape will be secured. You should be able to do this easily without pinning first. Use thread to match the prairie point fabric; a contrasting thread color is used here so that the tacking stitches are visible.

Prairie Point Coneflower

Make four prairie point units as in Steps 1 and 2 on pages 103 and 104, but **keep the double fold at the top of the background square** (away from your body).

Join these pieces into a Pinwheel block as you did for the Prairie Point Pinwheel, but this time, **place the double fold of each unit toward the outer edge of the star.**

2

Tip

Create just one 3-D cone and add an appliquéd frill for a jonquil, or artificial stamens and a long bias tape stem for a calla lily.

Place the sewn pinwheel on your work surface. Pick up a point and insert one finger between the double folds to spread them apart and create a hollow "cone." With your other hand, press down on the single fold so it aligns with the sewn seam. Smooth the prairie point into a kite shape. Gently finger-press the edges so they stay in place.

Assemble your blocks into a quilt top; layer, baste, and quilt it. **After quilting is complete, carefully hand tack the outer corners of the spread Prairie Points so they will hold their new shape.**

Crocus Star

1

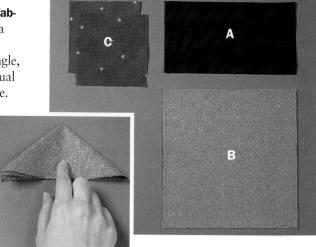

For this star, you will need three fabrics: a background rectangle (A), a square (B) with sides equal to the longest measurement of the rectangle, and two squares (C) with sides equal to the smallest side of the rectangle. We used a black 3½ × 6½-inch rectangle for A, a gold 6½-inch square for B, and two red 3½-inch squares for C.

To begin, fold the large B square in half diagonally twice to make a prairie point.

2

Place the A rectangle on your work surface, right side up. Align the long raw edges of the prairie point with the bottom long edge of the rectangle. **Secure the prairie point in place with a single pin.** This forms the center petal of the crocus.

3

Fold one of the C squares in half diagonally once, with the right side out. Position it on top of the A rectangle and the prairie point, **aligning the raw edges with a bottom corner of the rectangle.** Repeat with the second C square, folding it in half and **placing it over the opposite bottom corner.** To secure the pieces, stitch a security seam ⅛ inch from the bottom and side edges of the Crocus Star unit. The prairie point in the center will pop up through the folded corners, forming a crocus blossom.

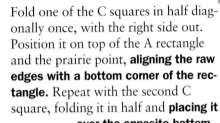

4

Consider "planting" a row of these crocuses as a flower border on your next quilt! Or, arrange them around a center square that's the same size as B. Fill in with corner squares the same size as C, **and you'll create a 12-pointed star block.** For the most dimensionality, avoid pressing the prairie point "petals" when you press the sewn seams of the block.

Tip

When joining the crocus stars to other blocks or patches, pin the tip of the center petal out of the way so it doesn't get sewn into the seam.

Dimensional *Patchwork*

While Bow Ties and other examples of three-dimensional piecing have been around since the 1920s, they still give a new look to your piecing. With these techniques, you include additional pieces of fabric—sometimes folded into interesting shapes—within the layers you're stitching together. These extras pop out from the seams, giving wonderful texture to the surface of your quilt. Try both the Bow Tie and its cousin, the On-Point Center Square, to make your next quilt a real attention-getter.

Getting Ready

Choose two fabrics that have high contrast. For the Bow Tie, you'll need five same-size squares: two of the background fabric and three for the tie. For the On-Point Center Square, you'll need two fabrics: one for the four background squares, and one contrasting fabric for the center square. Prewash and press your fabrics.

It's handy to use a ¼-inch patchwork foot or tape along the needle plate to make it easy to sew a consistent ¼-inch seam.

Be prepared to actually make these three-dimensional blocks as you read through the directions. As with origami (paper folding), these fabric manipulations are best understood by holding and folding the actual pieces in your hands. It really helps to be able to view the pieces from various perspectives, instead of just the one shown in each photograph.

3-D Bow Tie Blocks

Note that in the examples shown here, a blue print is used for the bow tie, and a tan print is used for the background. Start with the bow tie knot: **Fold a square of the bow tie fabric in half, horizontally, with the right side out.** Place a background square right side up on a work surface. Position the folded knot square on top of the background square so that the long raw edges align at the top and the fold is across the middle of the background square. **Place a second bow tie fabric square on top, right side down, aligning all the edges with the background square and sandwiching the folded knot fabric between the two squares.**

1

2

Pin the layers together along one short side of the knot fabric. Sew, using a scant ¼-inch seam, along the raw edge. Begin at the edge that has four layers, and sew a continuous seam to the end of the squares. **Halfway through your seam, fold back the top fabric and check that your folded knot fabric hasn't shifted during sewing.** (Note that the fabric is shown to the right of the needle in order to clearly illustrate the folding back of layers.)

After sewing, **open the two squares out to one side.**

Tip

A Purple Thang or a tailor's awl helps to hold layers together when you're sewing; see "Resources" on page 126.

3

On the other end of the folded knot square, **place a background square and a bow tie square right sides together, sandwiching the knot between them.** Switch the positions of your bow tie and background fabrics so that the background squares are *not* next to each other on the same side of the folded knot square. Pin and sew these squares in place as before, **then open them out to the side.**

4

Grasp the raw edges of the folded knot square, and gently pull them away from each other so that you open and spread the knot. **Bring the two sewn seams at the ends of the knot together.** Coax both seam allowances toward the background fabric so the two seam allowances nest. **Pin the layers together in this position so they don't shift.**

Working with the left half of your bow tie block first (the half that will go through your machine first as you sew), align both raw edges of the knot fabric as you sandwich them between the background and bow tie squares. **Check that the folded edge of the knot is smooth and that it lies straight and flat for more than ¼ inch** so that you won't sew a tuck into your seam. Pin the fold in place and stitch along the raw edge, using a scant ¼-inch seam. **Stop sewing at the center with the needle down in the knot fabric.**

Raise your presser foot so that you have better access to the knot fabric. **Coax out the other side of the folded knot, check that there is more than ¼ inch to sew into the seam, and pin the edge of the fold in place.** Align the raw edges of the knot and the squares, and continue stitching the seam to the opposite edge.

Tip

Use a Purple Thang or a tailor's awl to gently pull the fold out and straighten it past ¼ inch.

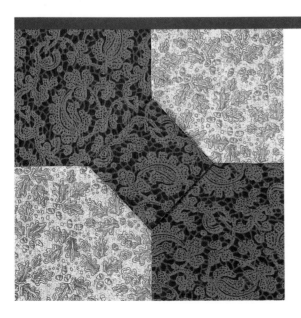

Open out the new seam, and your Bow Tie block is complete. Pressing with an iron will flatten the knot, lessening the 3-D effect. Instead, use the steam setting on your iron and let your fingers do the pressing. Working with the wrong side of the block face up, give the seam a shot of steam. Set your iron down and carefully work the seam allowances with your fingers to direct them to one side, as desired. This allows you to manipulate the seam allowances without compressing the 3-D effect of your patchwork. Repeat the shot of steam as needed.

DIMENSIONAL PATCHWORK

On-Point Center Square Blocks

1

This unit is similar in construction to the Bow Tie block, but gives you a 3-D square within a square.

You'll need four background squares and one center square. **Choose your fabrics and cut the background squares as directed in "What You'll Need" on page 109. Then cut the center square to twice the *finished size* of the background squares, plus ½ inch for seam allowances.** For example, if your background squares are cut to 3½ inches, cut your center square to 6½ inches (3 × 2 = 6 inches, plus ½ inch for seam allowances).

Tip

Your finished On-Point Center Square block will be the same size as your cut center square, minus ½ inch for seam allowances.

2

Fold the large center square in half horizontally, right side out. **Sandwich it between two pairs of background squares and sew the seams as described in Steps 1 through 3 on pages 109–110.**

Open out the folded center square, and sew the center seam as described in Steps 4 through 6 on pages 110–111.

3

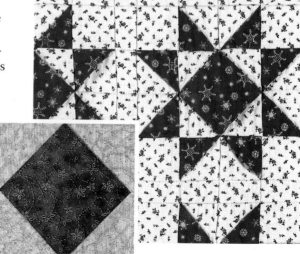

Open out the sewn seam, **and your On-Point Center Square is done.** Use steam to gently direct the seam allowances to one side and avoid flattening the block. Consider using this block as the center unit for another block, **such as a Sawtooth Star.** To make the star tips dimensional as well, follow the directions for the Crocus Star Block on page 106.

Learn to Tie a Bow Tie

Problem	Solution
The bow tie knot isn't smooth; the corners have little pinches or creases.	When catching the folded knot in the final stitching, be certain the folded edges are even with the patchwork and the fold is more than ¼ inch wide so you won't stitch in a pucker.

Skill Builder

Try one of these variations of the On-Point Center Square block.

❏ If you cut the center square a little smaller, it won't quite reach the seam allowances, showing background all around and giving the block a different look.

❏ Instead of four identical background squares, use two or even four different fabrics.

Try This!

Don't be afraid to use directional fabrics in your 3-D Bow Tie blocks.

If you want the lines in the knot to match the lines of the tie, fold it so the pattern runs in the opposite direction of your bow tie squares when you sandwich the knot. If you want the lines of the knot to run opposite those of the bow ends, fold the bow tie knot square so the pattern runs in the same direction as your bow tie squares when you sandwich the knot.

Or, if you want the knot in your bow tie to stand out from the tie (visually, in addition to dimensionally), substitute a contrasting fabric for the folded bow tie knot square.

DIMENSIONAL PATCHWORK

Making a tessellation is as easy as putting ducks in a row. With just a snip of the scissors and a flip of the wrist, a simple square becomes a more interesting shape—one that nests together with other, identical shapes. While the interlocking pieces are all the same, the quilt you create will be truly original, like the offbeat duck in Judy Doenias's design. Once you start designing and translating your designs into fabric, you'll discover that the possibilities will flow, and the process will go swimmingly!

Getting Ready

A tessellation is a single shape or several different shapes that make a pattern, covering an entire surface without gaps or overlap. The pieces fit together like a jigsaw puzzle and can repeat in any direction indefinitely. They range from the Tumbling Blocks design, a simple, one-shape tessellation, to the exquisitely drawn, complicated, and beautiful tessellations of the artist M. C. Escher.

The best way to become proficient at tessellations is to just try them out. Don't be afraid to follow your instincts and try something new and different.

Read through the chapter to design your own one-shape tessellations. Start with colored, unlined index cards, cardstock, or any sturdy paper to cut into squares or rectangles. You can create thousands of different designs using the translation and rotation techniques below.

What You'll Need

Fabrics of your choice

Index cards or card stock

Pen or pencil

Paper scissors

Clear tape or masking tape

Colored pencils or markers

Graph paper

Ruler

Design wall

Sewing machine

Thread to match fabrics

Translation

1

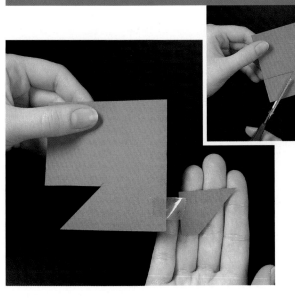

Design your own tessellations using 3-inch squares cut from 3 × 5 index cards. Start with one of the simplest forms of tessellation, called a translation. To create a translation, mark and cut a simple shape from one side of a square, and slide it across to the other side of the square. Following the example shown here, **mark two lines at a corner that meet to produce a trapezoid; cut out the shape.** Slide this shape across the square to a corresponding location on the opposite side. **Tape the shape in place.**

TESSELLATIONS: JUST DUCKY!

115

2

Trace your new shape onto a piece of paper several times, so the resulting shape repeats in an interlocking design. You've got a tessellation! Notice that these pieces tessellate, or fit together, to form straight rows, but the rows may be either lined up or staggered to form a pattern.

3

For a more complex translation, modify more than one side of your shape. **Cut an additional, different piece from the top, and slide it down to the same spot on the bottom; tape it in place.** As long as each cutout is replaced on the opposite side of the original shape, you have a translation. The more cutouts, the more interesting your shape becomes, but also the more difficult your design may be to piece. **Trace your new shape onto a piece of paper several times, so the resulting shape repeats in an interlocking design.**

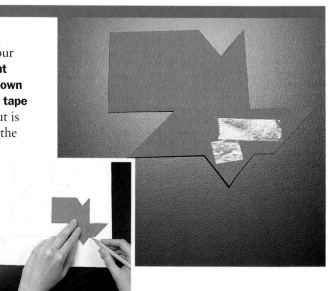

Rotation

1

Another form of tessellation is a rotation. For this design, you *turn* each cutout piece as you slide it across your original shape. The original shape shown here is a 2 × 3-inch rectangle. **Cut a shape or shapes from one side, then rotate them as you slide them across into their new positions on the other side.** Tape the cutouts into their new places.

To view the new tessellation, **trace your new, overall shape onto paper so that the repeating shape interlocks.**

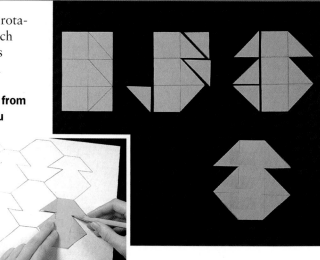

Another form of rotation takes the same cutout shape away from opposite sides of the original shape. Start with a 3-inch square. Cut out a small piece from one edge or corner, and rotate the square 180 degrees (so it's upside down). Place the cutout in the same position it was in on the original side, trace it, **and then cut out along the traced lines.**

Again, **your resulting shape will interlock with its repeated forms** when traced several times onto a piece of paper.

Translating It into Fabric

Once you have created a tessellating shape you would like to turn into a quilt, it's time to work on creating an easily pieced pattern. **Draw or trace your index card pattern onto graph paper, redrawing the lines slightly as necessary to make the overall shape fit onto whole squares in the grid.** (This will make it easier to piece.) Then, to get a good idea of the overall design, **repeat the interlocking shape in a smaller scale on graph paper,** covering an entire page.

Tip

Photocopy the page so you can create plenty of variations on your design.

Using colored pencils or markers, color in the shapes, experimenting with a variety of designs and shadings until you find one that is pleasing to you. Use colors that represent the fabrics you will use to divide your shape into smaller sections. Or, combine shapes to make larger tessellating designs.

TESSELLATIONS: JUST DUCKY!

3

Tip

For a jagged edge that preserves the sharp points, use an envelope finish instead of traditional binding (see page 25).

Pick your favorite design to make in fabric. **Mark the edges of your quilt design with straight, bold lines.** You may need to truncate parts of the shapes around the edges if you want straight outer edges on your quilt.

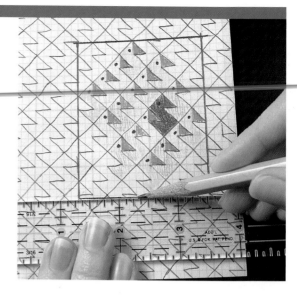

4

Tip

Tape pieces of graph paper together, if necessary, to enlarge your drawing to a workable scale.

Enlarge your design on graph paper so that you can easily see all your shapes and areas. **Color the enlarged drawing.**

Many tessellated designs are easily pieced in vertical, horizontal, or diagonal rows; the rows are sewn together to complete the design area. Examine your design to see which direction your quilt will be most easily pieced in, and what sections are most easily joined. **Draw piecing lines, combining areas of the same, adjacent color into one patch.** Draw additional lines as needed, dividing areas to avoid setting in seams.

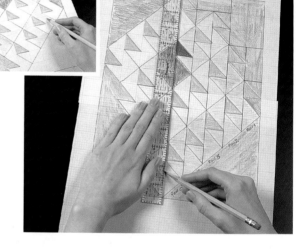

5

Tip

For easiest counting and scaling up, use graph paper that has ¼-inch squares.

Determine the finished size you want to make your quilt. Since you translated and enlarged your design on graph paper, it's easy to scale up the size of each finished piece. First, decide on the overall dimension of a side, then divide by the number of graph paper squares to determine what measurement each square on the graph paper will represent. **Multiply that number by the number of squares in a shape, and you have the finished size for that shape.** Keep in mind that you want to end up with measurements in ¼-inch increments, and adjust your overall dimensions as needed.

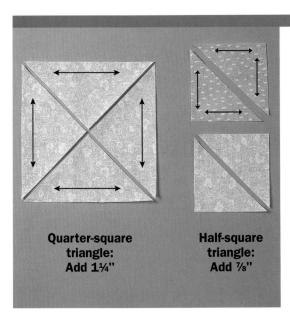

Quarter-square triangle: Add 1¼"   **Half-square triangle: Add ⅞"**

6

Cut patches so that the straight grain of the fabric falls along the outside of all your piecing rows. To cut square and rectangular patches, add ½ inch for seam allowances to the finished size on your drawing. Cut half-square triangles or quarter-square triangles according to your grain needs. **If a short side of a triangle falls along a main piecing line, cut a half-square triangle. If the long side of a triangle falls along a main piecing line, cut a quarter-square triangle.** Add ⅞ inch to the finished size of half-square triangles to determine the cut size of the parent square; add 1¼ inches for quarter-square triangles.

Tip

For shapes that don't lend themselves to rotary cutting, draw them onto template plastic, add ¼-inch seam allowances, and then trace them onto the fabric.

7

Place all your fabric patches on a design wall. Stand back and check your design from a distance. **Evaluate your fabric choices and make substitutions where you feel it is necessary to even out the design or to emphasize one aspect of it.** Once you are completely satisfied, sew the pieces together in rows, and then sew the rows together.

Tip

Have lots of extra coordinating fabrics and cut patches on hand to expand your design options.

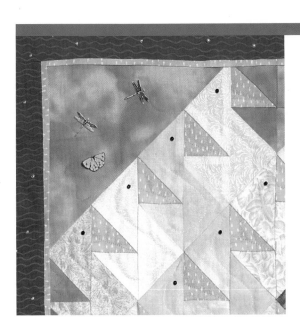

8

You don't need to cover the entire surface of the quilt top with your tessellations. **Set off a complex area with some plain background areas, like the triangles in the corners of Judy Doenias's quilt.** You might also repeat the tessellated shape on unpieced areas by way of your quilting stitches: Try using stitch outlines that echo the tessellated shape. Besides quilting, you may want to embellish your quilt to make a shape more recognizable. Buttons as eyes work well alongside the bright yellow-orange half-square triangle duck bills, making these tessellated shapes "read" more easily as a flock of ducks.

Innovative Piecing
Glossary

Bias. The stretchy, diagonal line of the fabric. True bias is at a 45-degree angle to the straight grain, but any off-grain cut may be referred to as a bias cut.

Color value. The relative lightness or darkness of any color, often referred to when discussing contrast.

Concave curve. An inward curve, like the outline left when you take a bite out of a cookie.

Convex curve. An outward curve, like a dome, or the outer edge of crust on a slice of pie.

Concave   Convex

Crosswise grain. The straight grain that runs perpendicular to the selvages.

Design wall. A flat, vertical surface, usually covered with flannel, felt, or batting, where quilt designs and fabric combinations can be easily auditioned.

Drafting. The process of drawing and designing a quilt block to fit a desired finished size.

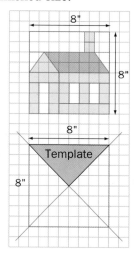

Foundation. A base material that stabilizes small or stretchy fabric patches during piecing. Patches are sewn directly onto the foundation, which is either removed (as with paper foundations) or left in the quilt (as with fabric foundations) once the entire unit is pieced.

Freezer paper. Found in the household supplies section of the supermarket, this plastic-coated paper sticks to fabric when pressed with an iron.

Graph paper. Gridded paper that can be used to draft quilt blocks and design quilts. Graph paper comes in a variety of grid sizes; ⅛-inch and ¼-inch grids work well for quilting purposes.

Jigsaw set. A quilt design containing a variety of blocks or other pieced units in assorted sizes. Units are assembled as a jigsaw puzzle is, by determining which pieces fit best in each position.

Lengthwise grain. The straight grain that runs parallel to the selvages.

Log Cabin block. A block constructed by adding strips around a center shape, traditionally a square.

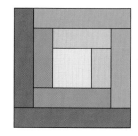

M

Monofilament. Very fine nylon thread, available in clear or smoke (dark gray) for use on light and dark fabrics, respectively, where it will be virtually invisible.

P

Panel. Strips sewn together to create "pieced fabric" that can be used as background, borders, or sashing, or can be cut into patches.

Perspective. A visual design element that shows relative distance or depth.

Photo transfer. The process of transferring a photograph onto fabric.

Prairie point. A square piece of fabric, folded diagonally in half twice, to create a triangle of fabric that looks the same on the front and back sides.

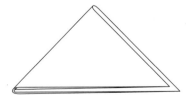

R

Registration lines. Short perpendicular lines drawn through sewing lines on templates or fabrics to aid in matching seams.

Rotation. A process in which a shape is turned as it is moved to a different location. When a shape moves by rotation, it is turned around a fixed point to its new location, like the hour hand on a clock face.

S

Sashing. Framing strips, also called lattice, that surround individual blocks or pieced units.

Scale. The relative size of designs, lines, elements, or motifs in a quilt or in individual fabric prints.

Small　　Medium　　Large

Security seam. A line of stitching that secures one piece of fabric to another to prevent shifting. About ⅛ inch from the raw edge, the security seam will be concealed within a standard ¼-inch sewing seam.

Set-in seam. A patch sewn into an L-shaped or V-shaped opening.

Shadowing. When seam allowances of dark fabrics show through a lighter fabric from underneath.

Square up. To straighten the edges of a block, row, or quilt top and make the corners true 90-degree angles, using a rotary cutter and acrylic ruler.

Stabilizer. A stiff or non-woven material that holds its shape and that of the fabrics sewn to it, preventing stretching or puckering.

Strip set. Two or more straight or curved strips of fabric sewn together along the lengthwise edges.

T

Template. An exact copy of a pattern piece, used as a guide for marking or cutting patches, or for positioning fabric.

Tessellation. A pattern of one or more repeating shapes that completely covers a surface without gaps or overlaps.

Three-dimensional piecing. Folded fabric pieces sewn into seams, but left free so they provide raised effects on the surface of the quilt.

Tone-on-tone print. Fabric that contains two values of the same color; it often reads as a solid.

Translation. A process in which shapes are moved without turning or inverting them. The shape is slid from one position to another along a straight line without changing its orientation.

without considering their colors.

Unfinished size. The measurement of a patch that includes a ¼-inch seam allowance along each side.

Value finder. A piece of translucent plastic, usually red, used to view the relative values of fabrics

Visual texture. The pattern or design printed on fabric that may provide interest or the illusion of dimension.

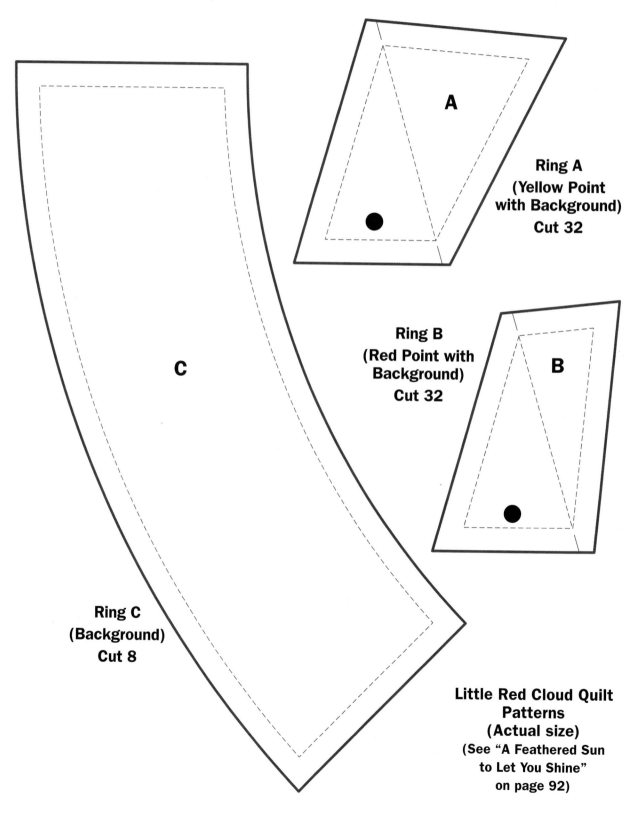

A

**Ring A
(Yellow Point
with Background)
Cut 32**

**Ring B
(Red Point with
Background)
Cut 32**

B

C

**Ring C
(Background)
Cut 8**

**Little Red Cloud Quilt
Patterns
(Actual size)
(See "A Feathered Sun
to Let You Shine"
on page 92)**

Acknowledgments

Quilt Artists

We gratefully thank the following quilt-makers who graciously permitted us to show their original designs in this book, and who provided samples, as well:

Sonya Lee Barrington, Small Work…Solids #30, 2000, on page 78

Karen Combs, Sunrise, 1995, on page 38

Judith Doenias, Be An Original, 2000, on page 114

Karen Eckmeier, Crescendo, 1998, on pages 4–5 and 96; Cross Currents, 1999, on page 84; Blueberry Pie à la Mode, 1999, on page 90

Janice Eggleston, Photo Fun, 2000, on page 23

Susan Else, Captured on Film, 1997, on page 24

John Flynn, Little Red Cloud, 1994, on page 92

Ellen Graf, Attic Treasure, 1998, on pages 2–3 and 10

Barbara Olson, Day One, 1995, on page 62

Jackie Robinson, Rubies & Other Jewels, 1998, on page 102; Pockets Full of Stardust, 1997, on page 108 (patterns available; see "Resources" on page 126)

Elizabeth Rosenberg, Strawberry Fields Forever, 1998, on page 44; The Ladies are Having a Really Bad Hair Day, 1998, on page 26; Skewed Hearts, 2000, on the cover and on page 33

Linda Dease Smith, Ours Will Be Cotton, 1997, on pages 20 and 126

Karen Costello Soltys, Drunkard's Path, 2000, on page 72

Carol Taylor, Wildfire, 1999, on page 14

Elsie Vredenburg, Cheboygan Crib Light I, II, and III, 2000, on page 56

Virginia A. Walton, Falling In Love With Curves I and II, 2000, on page 68 (patterns available; see "Resources" on page 126)

Darra Duffy Williamson, Wish You Were Here, 2000, on page 50

Cheryl Wittmayer, Starry Nites, 1995, on page 34 (pattern available; see "Resources" on page 126)

Samplemakers

In addition to the quiltmakers above, the following people made samples: Sarah Sacks Dunn, Eleanor Levie, and Carol Singer

Photography

Clark Martens is the photographer for Barbara Olson's quilt on page 62. The photo of Susan Else's quilt on page 24, bottom, is by Jamie Pennington, courtesy of P&B Textiles.

All other photographs are by John P. Hamel.

Art pottery on pages 34 and 78 is from the collection of Dana S. Dunn.

Supplies

American & Efird—Mettler threads, Signature machine quilting threads

Bernina of America—Virtuosa 150 sewing machine

Big Board—large ironing board

Byrne Sewing Connection—sewing machine extension trays

Clotilde—stiletto, silk pins, assorted notions

Fiskars—embroidery scissors, rotary cutters

Marcus Brothers, Inc.—fabrics

Olfa—rotary cutters

Omnigrid—acrylic rulers, cutting mats

P & B Textiles—fabrics

Rowenta—professional iron

Sonya Lee Barrington has been using the medium of quilts as her means of expression for 30 years. Her work is held in private collections and has been included in many solo and group exhibits, both juried and invitational. Formerly a college professor of textile arts, she currently teaches, lectures, and gives workshops. Sonya produces a line of hand-dyed and textured fabrics that she uses in her own work and markets to other quilters.

Karen Combs is a quilter, author, teacher, and designer who is known for her quilts of illusion. A teacher since 1989, she is in high demand as someone who encourages her students, makes learning fun, and makes the complex easy to understand. She is the author of *Optical Illusions for Quilters, 3-D Fun with Pandora's Box,* and *Combing Through Your Scraps.* In addition, Karen has appeared on the TV programs *Quilting from the Heartland* and *Simply Quilts,* and she has written numerous articles about her quilting techniques. She and her family live in Columbia, Tennessee.

Judy Doenias has been involved in crafts of one kind or another since childhood. She teaches in quilt shops and in adult education programs in New York City, and she lectures and gives workshops to quilt guilds. She is a member of the Manhattan Quilters, a small guild of professional quiltmakers; the Online Quilters, a group that meets daily on the Internet; and she is a founding member of the Quilting Judys, an international group of quilters who all share the same first name.

Karen Eckmeier is an artist whose medium has been quilting since 1996. Although her specialty is curved piecing, she also enjoys hand appliqué, beadwork, and fabric painting . . . any way to inject energy and movement into a quilt! Karen is highly prolific and exhibits her work in quilt shows and museums. She also does commissioned work, and her quilts have received numerous national and international awards. She teaches quilting classes at The Country Quilter in Somers, New York.

John Flynn is a former bridge builder who is now an internationally known quilter. In 1981, he combined his twentieth-century engineer's mind with quilting's nineteenth-century technology and began designing quilting frames. He now markets his lap- and machine-quilting frames, teaches classes, and designs and exhibits his award-winning quilts internationally, and he almost never builds a bridge. He lives in Billings, Montana.

Barbara Olson is an international award-winning quilt artist. She has been creating quilts for the last 14 years; for the last 6 of those years, making art quilts has been her passion. She is a native of Montana, and has developed a series of workshops and lectures for those interested in expanding their creativity. When she's not traveling to teach, her life in Billings, Montana, centers on her family and making dynamic quilts of spirit and energy.

Jackie Robinson is a teacher, designer, and the author of 12 books on quiltmaking. She has been active in the business since 1982, when she opened her first shop in a St. Louis suburb. In 1988 she moved to Durango, Colorado, where she opened Animas Quilts. Her work has been featured in several quilt magazines and she has appeared on *Simply Quilts* and *Kaye's Quilting Friends.*

Elizabeth Rosenberg has spent most of her life playing and working with fabric and thread. She became obsessed with exploring the outer limits of her sewing machine's capabilities, using it to quilt, couch, embellish, and add flourish to her quilts. She teaches free-motion machine quilting and embellishment techniques, and through her company, Inventing Tradition, she also designs and distributes quilt patterns featuring images of Jewish tradition.

Karen Costello Soltys has been quilting since 1979, when she took her first quilting class at a local fabric shop. She is a former quilt book editor and is now a garden book editor for Rodale Inc. In her spare time, she still enjoys making quilts and wallhangings, taking classes, traveling to quilt shows, and browsing through all the quilt publications she can get her hands on—when it isn't gardening season, that is.

Carol Taylor is a quilt artist and teacher who has been quilting since 1993. She has created over 223 quilts in her short career, and she is a popular teacher in the Upstate New York area. A teacher by degree and outgoing by nature, she has been a recruiter since 1981 and owns her own business, Taylor Search Associates Inc., recruiting professional salespeople. She is thrilled to have been juried into Quilt National '99, to have had her quilts win numerous awards at 1999 and 2000 juried quilt shows, and to be included in many art quilt gallery exhibitions.

Elsie Vredenburg is probably best known for her pictorial pieced quilts, which are often combined with elements of traditional patchwork designs. Elsie's quilts have appeared in many national and international quilt shows, including American Quilter's Society, National Quilting Association, National Patchwork Association, Quilt Expo Europa, Quilters' Heritage Celebration, Quilt America, and American/International Quilters' Association. They have also appeared in *Quilter's Newsletter Magazine, Lady's Circle Patchwork Quilts, Quilting Today,* and *Traditional Quiltworks.*

Virginia A. Walton is the inventor of the Creative Curves Quilting System, which substitutes curves for half-square or half-rectangle triangles. She is a specialist in sewing machine techniques, in particular piecing curves without pins, and in the use of fabric in all its variety and colors to create the effects desired in a quilt. She has been teaching for approximately 18 years throughout the United States and has presented workshops and lectures to quilt guilds, festivals, and shows throughout the country. Virginia's original blocks and quilts have been featured in many quilt magazines. She is a frequent guest on *Lap Quilting with Georgia Bonesteel* and Kaye Wood's *Quilting With Friends* television series.

Darra Duffy Williamson collected quilts long before she began making them, and she still considers the nineteenth-century scrap quilt one of her greatest sources of inspiration. She is the author of *Sensational Scrap Quilts* and has written numerous magazine articles. She has spent the past few years exploring improvisational-style piecing and collage techniques, and much of her recent work reflects this interest. Darra is much in demand, both in the United States and abroad, for her informative and entertaining lectures and workshops. When not traveling, she quilts in her home in the Blue Ridge Mountains of North Carolina.

Cheryl Wittmayer is an award-winning fiber artist, and she has taught a wide range of classes for over 20 years. She has been a lecturer and quilt show judge, and she has written for *Ladies Circle Patchwork Quilts* magazine. Currently, Cheryl concentrates her time on her quilt pattern company, Sew Be It. She markets her original designs as patterns, offering an eclectic mix ranging from primitive folk art to an elegant and contemporary look. Cheryl lives in Billings, Montana.

Animas Quilts
Jackie Robinson
P.O. Box 693
Durango CO 81302
Phone: (970) 247-4549
Fax: (970) 247-2569
E-mail:
    AnimasQuiltsPublishing@
    Animas.com
Web site: www.animas.com
Books, patterns, tools

Sonya Lee Barrington
837 47th Avenue
San Francisco, CA 94121
Phone: (415) 221-6510
E-mail: slbstudio@jps.net
Hand-dyed fabrics

Clotilde
B3000
Louisiana, MO 63353
Phone: (800) 772-2891
Web site: www.clotilde.com
*Rotary cutting supplies,
value-finders, assorted tools,
sewing notions*

Creative Curves
Virginia A. Walton
3825 Camino Capistrano NE
Albuquerque, NM 87111
Phone: (505) 293-2903
Fax: (505) 294-1979
E-mail:
    info@creativecurves.com
Web site:
    www.creativecurves.com
*Creative Curves & Ellipse
rulers, books, patterns, and
videos*

Flynn Quilt Frame Company
1000 Shiloh Overpass Road
Billings, Montana 59106
    John Flynn's Step-By-Step
    Feathered Sun and other
    books, quilting frames,
    template kits

Little Foot, Ltd.
798 Terrace Ave
P.O. Box 1027
Chama, NM 87520
Phone: (800) 597-7075
    or (505) 756-1865
Fax: (505) 756-1512
Web site: www.littlefoot.net
Purple Thang

P & B Textiles, Inc.
E-mail: pandbtexsf@aol.com
*Naturescapes, Animals
fabric collections*

Sew Be It
3108 65th Street SW, R#1
Billings MT 59106
Phone: (406) 656-4515
E-mail: cherylwitt@imt.net
Patterns

Skydyes
P.O. Box 370116
West Hartford, CT 06137
Phone: (203) 232-1429
    *Hand-painted, one-of-
    a-kind fabrics*

Elsie Vredenburg
P.O. Box 301
Tustin, MI 49688
(enclose a SASE)
E-mail: elf@netonecom.net
Web site:
    www.netonecom.net/~elf/
    *Patterns for lighthouse and
    barn quilts*

Index

A

Angles, topstitched, 91
Appliqué, pieced
    applying to background, 48
    background for, 48, 49
    color variety in, 49
    design transfer, 45–46
    piecing, 46–48
    turning under edges, 48, 49
Appliqué, reverse, 75
Appliqué foot, 75
Arches
    cutting, 98–99
    piecing, 99–101
    templates for, 97–98, 101
Attic Windows,
    completing quilt top, 41–43
    depth in, 39, 43
    fabrics for, 40, 43
    piecing, 39–41

B

Basting glue, 48
Beach umbrellas, 55
Beads, as embellishments, 37
Bed-size quilts, 12
Bias edges
    handling, 18, 52
    sizing spray for, 40
    staystitching, 29, 54, 82
Blocks. *See also specific blocks*
    curve-pieced, 82
    enlarging and reducing, 11–12
    inconsistent sizes in, 23
    miniature, as center square, 13
    skewed, 27–33
Borders
    bias-cut, 18
    checkerboard, 63–67
    curve-pieced, 82
    for star point quilt, 37
    strip-pieced, 18
Bow Tie block
    Drunkard's Path variation, 76
    3-D, 109–11, 113

C

Calla lily, prairie point, 106
Captured on Film quilt, 24
Checkerboard border
    color gradation in, 67

drafting, 63–64
    piecing, 65–66
Color gradations, 67
Color matching, 18, 43, 65
Colors
    auditioning, 15
    blending, 16
    in pieced appliqué, 49
    setting strips for, 22
    topographical effects of, 90
Color theory, 15
Color value
    depth and, 43, 55
    finding, 39, 85
Compass Star, prairie point, 105
Computers, sizing designs with,
    11, 58
Concentric shapes, 55
Coneflower, prairie point, 106
Couching, 77
Crocus star, 106–7
Cropping guides, 57
Curves
    concave, 99
    cutting, 79–80, 83, 86–87, 98
    Drunkard's Path units, 73–77
    embellishing, 77
    Flying Geese Pinwheel, 71
    pinning, 100
    pressing, 91, 100
    stitching, 100
    strip-pieced, 79–82
    topstitched, 85–91
    triangle squares, 69–70
Cutting mats
    cutting curves on, 79, 86
    as piecing aid, 81
    as tracing aid, 74
Cutting techniques
    curves, 79–80, 83, 86–87, 98
    long strips, 16, 83
    safety, 79
    slipping fabric, 83
    small pieces, 40
    stretch prevention, 40
    uneven cuts, 83

D

Depth
    in Attic Windows, 39, 43
    in landscape panels, 55

Design wall
    making, 16
    using, 22, 23, 35, 119
Diagonal effects, 12
Directional fabrics
    for Bow Tie blocks, 113
    for skewed designs, 32
Double Four Patch block, 12
Drunkard's Path unit
    making templates, 74
    piecing, 74–77
    sizing, 73
    variations on, 76

E

Easy Tear stabilizer, 77
Embellishments
    for curves, 77
    for landscape panels, 55
    for star point quilt, 37
    for tessellations, 119
Enlarging and reducing, 11–12
Envelope finish, 25
Evening Star block, 13

F

Fabrics
    for Attic Windows, 43
    hand-dyed, 21
    hand-painted, 40
    theme, 21, 23, 43
Feathered Sun, 93–95
Finishing techniques, 25
Flying Geese block, skewed, 31–32
Flying Geese pinwheel, curved, 71
Fool's Puzzle block, 76
Foundation piecing, alternative to,
    28
Four Patch block
    prairie point, 104
    variations on, 11–12
Freezer paper
    appliqué, 46
    for designing, 31
    pressing, 46, 98
    templates, 60, 64, 98
Fusible web, 49

G

Glue, basting, 48
Grain lines, marking, 60, 97

H

Hand-quilting techniques, 36
Harvest Moon block, 76
Heart block, skewed, 33

J

Jigsaw sets, 23–24
Jonquil, prairie point, 106

L

Landscape panels
    depth in, 55
    designing, 51–52
    embellishing, 55
    piecing, 52–54
Lighting, 39
Log Cabin blocks
    rose design from, 30
    skewed, 30–31
Log Cabin sets, 21–23

M

Marking techniques, 41, 99
Miniblocks, 13

N

Needles, machine, 43
Nine Patch block, skewed, 29

O

On-Point Center Square block
    112, 113

P

Patches, curve-pieced, 82
Patchwork, dimensional
    Bow Tie block, 3-D, 109–11,
        113
    On-Point Center Square
        block, 112–13
Patchwork foot, 109
Photo Fun quilt, 23
Photographs, as design tool, 17, 19
Photographs, in quilt design
    design transfer, 58
    making pattern, 59–60
    piecing, 60–61
    tracing photos, 57–58
Pinning techniques
    curves, 100
    for easy pin removal, 81, 87
Pinwheels
    Flying Geese, curved, 71
    prairie point, 104
Polka Dots block, 76
Prairie points
    basic, 103
    compass star, 105
    coneflower, 106
    crocus star, 106–7
    defined, 103
    pinwheels, 104

Pressing
    Bow Tie blocks, 111
    curves, 91, 100
    freezer paper, 46, 98
Purple Thang, 110, 111
Puss in the Corner block, 13

Q

Quilters' GluTube, 48
Quilt tops, recycling, 19

R

Reversal technique, for strip sets,
    17
Ridges, 89–90
Rippling Water block, 76
Rose design, from Log Cabin, 30
Rotary cutters, safety with, 79
Rotation (tessellation), 116–17
Rulers, for curves, 69–71

S

Sashing, pieced, 24
Sawtooth block, 13
Sawtooth Star block, skewed,
    32–33
Scraps, using, 18, 53, 75, 77
Seam allowances, sizing blocks
    and, 13
Seams
    construction, 103
    puckered, 67
    security, 103
    set-in, 24
    stitching techniques, 70, 109
Settings
    jigsaw, 23–24
    Log Cabin, 21–23
    for multicolor blocks, 22
Shadow-through, 67
Shoo Fly block, 13
Sizing spray, cutting and, 40
Skewing
    basic, 27–28
    directional fabrics for, 32
    Flying Geese, 31–32
    Heart, 33
    Log Cabin, 30–31
    Nine Patch, 29
    Sawtooth Star, 32–33
    staystitching and, 29
Stabilizers
    for appliqué, 48
    for puckers, 77
Star points, from rectangles, 35–37
Staystitching, 29, 54, 82
Stitching techniques
    curves, 100
    over pins, 99
    seams, 70, 109
Stitch lengths
    for appliqué, 47, 75

    for curves, 81
    for topstitching, 87
Stitch-n-Tear stabilizer, 48
Stretch prevention, for bias edges
    handling, 18, 52
    sizing spray, 40
    staystitching, 29, 54
Strip sets
    borders, 18
    curved, 79–82
    cutting, 16, 83
    for Feathered Sun, 93–94
    landscape, 51–55
    left over, using, 19
    rainbow, 15–18
Sulky Totally Stable, 64

T

Tailor's awl, 110, 111
Templates. *See also specific
    projects and blocks*
    vs. foundation piecing, 28
    freezer paper, 60, 64, 98
    problems with, 67
Tension, adjusting, 77
Tessellations
    cutting, 119
    defined, 115
    designing quilt, 117–18
    embellishing, 119
    piecing, 119
    shapes for, 115–17
Thread
    for appliqué, 48, 75
    color matching, 18, 43, 65
    as embellishment, 77
    monofilament, puckers from, 77
    for seams, 43
Topographical effects
    with color, 90
    ridges, 89–90
    valleys, 88–89
Topstitched angles, 91
Topstitched curves
    cutting, 86–87
    piecing with, 90
    ridges in, 89–90
    stitching, 87–88
    valleys in, 88–89
Tracing techniques, 57–58, 60,
    74
Translation (tessellation), 115–16
Triangle squares, curved, 69–70
Triple Four Patch block, 12

V

Valleys, 88–89
Value finders, 39, 85

Y

Yardage, from topstitched curves,
    90

INDEX

Quilting Styles

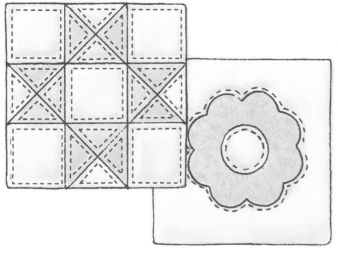

Outline Quilting

Echo Quilting

Single

Double

Crosshatch or Grid Quilting

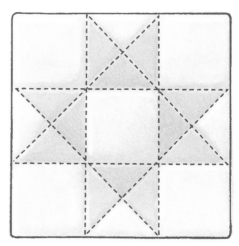

In the Ditch Quilting

Stipple Quilting

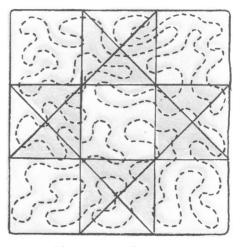

Meander Quilting